What people are saying:

"*Detroit Fairy Tales* is a stunner of a ⸺ ⸺ Elisa Sinnett has summoned a glittering darkness, bleak, beautiful, mesmerizing and utterly unforgettable."—Junot Díaz, Pulitzer Prize-winning author of *The Brief Wondrous Life of Oscar Wao*

"*Detroit Fairy Tales* is real, it's beautiful, it's magical, it's painful like the city we both know and fucking love. Fiction? Nonfiction? Truth? Clever lies? Like a classic song that stays in your head this book both evokes memories and creates new memories."— Owólabi Aboyade (Will See), Detroit MC and cultural organizer

"A stunning collection by an exciting new voice in experimental memoir, Elisa Sinnett's *Detroit Fairy Tales* is a devastating love letter to the indomitable soul of a grand American city—a soul that can never be foreclosed or gentrified. What is remembered lives. And long live Detroit in Sinnett's powerful debut."—Ariel Gore, author of *The End of Eve*, winner of the New Mexico-Arizona Book Award, and founder of *Hip Mama Magazine*

"Clear-eyed heartfelt smart staccato funny terrible: *Detroit Fairy Tales* is all of this, and Elisa Sinnett's voice is a wonder."—Kathe Koja, award-winning author of *The Cipher*, *Under the Poppy*, and *Dark Factory*

"More than a story about growing up in a certain time and place, Eilsa Sinnett's *Detroit Fairy Tales* explores how time and place are just as important to a narrative as the people experiencing their lives within it. ... With precise storytelling and captivating language, *Detroit Fairy Tales* is an enthralling read that considers who we are by looking at where we come from and how the past shapes our future." —Chelsey Clammer, author of *Circadian* and *BodyHome*

Trade paperback ISBN 978-1-7339763-8-1
e-book ISBN 978-1-7339763-9-8

Flexible Press LLC
Editor William E Burleson
Copy editor Vicki Adang,
Mark My Words Editorial Services, LLC
Original art copyright Debranne Dominguez
Author photo by Nora Romelia Sinnett

Detroit Fairy Tales is dedicated to Ariel Gore,
the hippest mama of all, and to Jamie,
wherever you are.

Detroit Fairy Tales is a work of speculative memoir, as in this is a story of me in my own fictional world. I start telling a true story, then veer off into fiction out of fear, invention, or a desire to breathe life into what's been erased. People in my life have been combined, compressed, and altered beyond recognition. As a result, these stories are the fairy-tale version of my life. — Elisa Sinnett

Contents

Coming of Age in the Murder City: The 1980s 1

The Lives of Girls and Boys: The 1960s–1970s 41

Family of Origin: The 1950s... 73

Independence Day—Young Adulthood: The 1990s 103

Elegy for Our Home in Detroit: Y2K........................... 133

Coming of Age in the Murder City:
The 1980s

White People Steps

Some Friendly Advice

Bicycles

The View from Senator Street

Lunchtime at Cass Park

Meant to Disturb

Darling Frankie

White People Steps

Elisa, 1980

This morning I woke up in the White world. Detroit, Michigan. 7 Mile Road. West side. 1980. We live on parallel streets going from east to west, starting at the Detroit River, ratcheting up towards 8 Mile and the suburbs in one-mile steps. Like bicycle spokes, larger avenues start downtown at the hub and stretch far, far away to better places like Chicago, where people have briefcases and ride the train. Placement along the gridlines plots a person's destiny, and we Detroiters are supposed to stay put.

At school, on the White people steps, we say people are Black. White. Mexican. I know there are some mixed-race kids, but I don't know what they do. One of them was the Homecoming queen this year. She was beautiful in her satin gown from Hudson's. I saw her picture in the Sunday *Detroit Free Press*.

For us, nobody else exists. At our school, Black and White don't mix very much unless they are in school activities together and take turns being the most popular kids in the school. Our school, Cass Tech, is famous for its music program. My sister is in the singing group, The Madrigals, just like Diana Ross used to be. They get dressed up on performance day, but my sister doesn't own a skirt and only has one bra, so she can't get into uniform for the musical performances. She has to pretend that she "forgot" her show bag at home, and Ms. Terry always lends her a school dress without a word. You have to know that people never used the word "hillbilly" or "White trash" on us, but we knew not to try to get too close to the Black kids. We wanted to save ourselves the embarrassment of the brush-off, the rejection.

The Southwest side is more my style. People are over all these rules about who is cool and who is not because their parents are in the union and strike together at the factory. Sometimes we have the car, and we drive people home over to the Southwest side, but most of the time we are on foot or on the bus.

Finding a guy is impossible at school because I'm not allowed to date Black kids, even if they'd look at me in my hand-me-down clothes and washed-out pale skin. I have to skip and go over to the Southwest side where all the cute White and Mexican boys are. So it's time to move away from la door and e-skip-iar la school because we need to find boyfriends.

"Elisa!" I turn and see Lainey. She's already got a cigarette lit for me. "Tony's looking at you again." I look over at Tony Racovides.

He's cute. Too bad, I think. "His hands are too sweaty," I tell her.

Lainey laughs. "You didn't seem to mind after practice yesterday."

I laugh. "Mayyyyybe..."

The rest of the crowd on the White people steps disperses when the first bell rings. Pretty soon Bonnie and Clyde, the security guards, will be out here chasing us all inside, and it'll be too late to make a break over to the Southwest.

"Let's get out of here."

Lainey and I pool our resources after we are well away from the school and Bonnie and Clyde's stack of detention pads. We have enough change for the bus or for two Top Hat hamburgers each. Neither one of us has eaten breakfast, so we start walking, past downtown, past the Michigan Central Train Station, under the viaduct, and onto West Vernor Highway. The Amtrak trains clink overhead.

We work on our school spirit for the pep rally, singing and shouting, "From east to west, Cass Tech is the best..." as we walk through the cement-arched tunnel, jogging past the cave-like slit where people sneak over to Canada through the train tunnel under the river. Now we're officially on the Southwest side—just two blocks from the Ambassador Bridge to Canada, but still two miles from Lainey's house. My feet hurt, and I'm hot and thirsty. Brown leaves rustle around our sneakers, and it's feeling cold and damp.

We hear the car before we see it; a rusty brown '72 Dodge Duster with a white stripe pulls over to the curb and stops. Lainey and I look at each other. "Joaquin!"

We run over to climb in. Joaquin Davis wears a tight white T-shirt, and his muscular, golden-brown arm drapes casually over the back of the passenger seat. Joaquin is Mexican, but he speaks hardly any Spanish after the teachers tried to beat it out of him. Now he and his parents can barely understand each other.

Lainey jumps in first, so I squeeze in next to her. "Lucky," I mutter at her. Joaquin is yummy. She laughs and shifts toward him.

"What the hell, you walked all the way from school?"

"Yeah, we're starving," Lainey says.

"I'll take you to ACE Convenience then."

Lainey tucks herself under his outstretched arm. "Thanks, Joaquin."

He doesn't object as we pile up our snacks for him to pay, but we pick out the cheapest off-brand Cheetos and grape pop so he won't think we're trying to use him.

Joaquin drives us deeper into the neighborhood toward Lainey's house, rattling over the tracks. I'm glad we aren't walking. As we pass under the viaducts, I hear the Dodge engine's echo vibrating like a jet taking off. On the other side, the car chugs around the Vernor Avenue curve as Lainey lays her head on Joaquin's shoulder. I roll my eyes at Romeo and Juliet and watch the side mirror instead. Joaquin and I see the flashing red lights at the same time.

"Oh shit!" he says as he pulls over.

I try to sit up straight and pull Lainey up. Joaquin rolls down the window, then stares straight ahead, both hands gripping the wheel. I follow his lead and roll down the window, then sit with my hands folded, looking straight ahead. Lainey's hand grips mine, fingernails digging into my palm. I feel the presence of the blond policeman at my side, but it's the other White officer who speaks to Joaquin.

"License and registration." He pauses. "Don't you know all passengers are required to wear seatbelts?" Joaquin groans, soft enough for only us to hear.

We're afraid of what's going to happen next, but it's Joaquin who gets pulled out of the car, no matter how slowly he moves or how carefully he follows instructions.

"This insurance is expired. Will you step out of the car?"

I start to move, but the officer on my side puts up his hand to stop me. He moves around to the other side of the car where the first officer is bending Joaquin over the car, patting him down, then taking him back to the squad car, and shoving him in the back.

The officer is back at my window.

"Your licenses?" We hand over our student IDs. "Tenth grade?"

I nod, look down. Lainey gulps and nods.

"How old are you?"

"Fifteen." It's like we're twin parrots, chirping out the same answers.

"Has this man been supplying you with alcohol? Did he try to rape you? Why aren't you in school?" The officer asks his questions rapid-fire.

"No! I...He didn't..." I try to speak, but the officer cuts me off.

"Stay here." He goes back to the squad car with Joaquin and the other police officer.

I bow my head. We're getting Joaquin into so much trouble. Long minutes pass, and I have to go pee. Finally the first officer comes up to the window.

"Get out of the car," he says. Lainey and I tumble out, then stand shakily, our legs half asleep from sitting in the cramped front seat for so long.

The officer doesn't seem interested in us at all. Instead, he turns toward the tow truck backing up and hooking to Joaquin's bumper. Lainey is frozen in place, but I'm hopping back and forth, wondering where I can find a bathroom. The officer seems surprised to see us still standing there. He steps in closer.

"You girls Mexican?" he asks.

"Um, no?" Lainey answers.

"Look, girls," the officer says. "Go back to school, and don't get in cars with Mexicans."

We stand there like two mute dummies by the viaduct as the squad car pulls away, Joaquin in the back seat, spine erect, staring straight ahead.

"Shit," Lainey says. "We left our Cheetos in the car."

Some Friendly Advice

Detroit Winter, 1977

In grade school I sat next to the girl who would be the second known victim of the Oakland County Child Killer. Jill squinted like she needed glasses, and she never talked in class. I never even heard her ask to borrow a pencil. I might not have remembered her at all if her family hadn't moved away after our fifth-grade year to get away from all the danger in Detroit.

Jill Robinson was 12 years old when she was murdered. When the police figured out there was a serial child killer, the whole community was on alert. We were terrified of middle-aged White men driving blue Gremlins with a white swoosh. We played Hit the Ground.

Timothy King. Timothy King. We prayed for Timothy King, who would be the last boy killed. We prayed for Timothy King to come home safe. "In the name of the Father and the Son and the Holy Spirit. Jesus please bring home Timothy King safely to his family. Please bring Timothy home safely. Please, mister, have mercy. Do not kill Timothy like you killed Jill. Please let Timothy King go, mister."

He did not.

We were taught strategies to evade kidnappers. "Be alert at all times. If those men in that truck try to talk to you and offer you a ride, smile and tell them, 'No, thanks, I'm home.' And walk right up to the house like it's yours."

My sister did that when she was in seventh grade. Went straight into the back yard from Fairfield to Muirland. Hopped the fence. Ran through to the next street. Made sure they didn't see her at the corner. Ran straight home. That was the White men. White men tried to stick you in their car and take you somewhere and kill you like they did Jill and Timothy and Kristine and Mark.

Black men came right up on you. Dad said, "Give them your stuff if they ask for it." I did that even when they were boys my own age and I knew that wasn't a pistol in their jacket but their finger pointed at me. They were called muggers. "Don't fight back. It's only stuff," Dad said. "Don't die for stuff ever. You're worth more to me, darling." We walked together in groups to school to stop the Northwest Rapist who came into homes and raped the moms. White boys gave their girlfriends drugs, then tried to rape them. Black boys said, "Can I get with that?" And if you said no, but with a smile, they said, "OK, little mama."

Here is some advice I learned over the years. It's a wonder that my own teen girls don't understand half of it. They think I worry too much, but that makes me worry.

Don't do drugs, or you'll get it. Stay on the block, or boys will steal your bikes. Learn how to fight. Practice dog fighting with your big sister. Get in fistfights with boys like your sister does. When you see your Canadian cousins, throw apples, hard, at their heads. Throw them off the hay mow. Keep playing even if your head is bleeding. At home, play tackle football without equipment. Play roller hockey in the street. Stick your opponent and don't cry when they push you over. Play with blood soaking down into your socks unless there's a big flap on your knee and you can't get all the gravel out. Ring doorbells and run away from the angry dads screaming from their porches with a rifle in their hands. Ride your bike and give guys the finger when they try to grab you from their car. Ride fast. Ride faster. Learn to ride the bus downtown. Sit near the front so the bus driver will say something when the men try to touch you. Beat one big girl, bad, at wrestling. Knock her down once in a while for fun while people are watching. Then you don't have to fight again. Ever.

When Mom pulls a knife on you, laugh at her, then go to your room and hyperventilate. And in your last year of teenagerhood, when your mom assaults and chokes you, fight back. Get up and breathe. Live. And this time, don't carry that woman's voice around with you, even after she's dead.

Just some friendly advice.

Bicycles

Elisa, 1979

I want to ride my bicycle. It's a deep green Schwinnn Varsity, drop handle, purchased used with my newspaper route money from a kid from the suburbs selling it in the *Tradin' Times* magazine. Now I have no limits, just the length of the day; it varies a lot in Michigan. I'll admit to e-skip-iando la school and looking for boyfriends instead of being a lady and curling my hair and letting them choose me. As for math class, seventh hour? I do math all afternoon instead. Detroit is 656 feet above sea level, flat and green and great for riding. Detroit is at 42 degrees latitude; that's almost halfway between the equator and the North Pole. When it gets cold in the winter, I ride with socks over my gloves. I can ride with no hands. I can ride around Belle Isle nineteen times. I can ride a straight distance of 60 miles, to Pontiac and back after school and get home before dark in the spring when the days are long. In the summer I have to work at the Detroit Golf Club, and I'm tired, so my reach is only 25 miles all together. Detroit has an area of 140 square miles, but I'm not into the whole city. I'm more of a direct north and south kind of girl. Down to Fort Wayne and the Detroit River, up to Pontiac. Then east to Belle Isle and round and round. I guess I have a lot of energy, but nowhere to burn it, though soccer season slows me down, and now Lainey and her friends. I spend a lot of time alone, thinking. It's like doing laps in a swimming pool, but I can only swim for about an hour, and my longest bike ride was about six hours without stopping. It's a lot of time to think, and truth is, I don't need school or a boyfriend or crazy friends. My crazy gets all bottled up and comes out sideways when I'm with them. I'm better off alone. I want to ride my bike.

The View from Senator Street

Elisa, 1981

Back when I believed in God, He was Irish Catholic, like me. My family prayed to Him at the dinner table and every night before bed. Our existence from September to June was confined to the leafy, square-mile island of Detroit's University District: 6 Mile to the south, 7 Mile to the north, Livernois to the west, and the Detroit Golf Club to the east. We rarely left our neighborhood, but every summer Mom, Dad, my five sisters, me, and Faygo the dog piled into the yellow Ford Econoline van with no seatbelts and drove up Gratiot to the Blue Water Bridge. We escaped the pull of the magnet buried deep in the Detroit River that keeps Detroiters like us from traveling past the city's northern redlining boundary of 8 Mile and heading for Canada.

The popular kids who dominated Catholic grade school were the unfriendly progeny of automobile executives, good Catholic families eating their daily bread and getting rich on account of the Big Three auto companies. My classmates were real Detroiters; they had concrete and metal dreams, backlit by fluorescent light bulbs, bright and unforgiving. The boys ruled the safety patrol, the altar boys and the playground, law and order, right-minded citizens in training. In class, I basked under the watchful eyes of the nuns, but as soon as we escaped their gaze, the social order resumed. In gym class, flinty blue eyes passed over me when it was time to pick teams for dodgeball.

"Your shoes are boy shoes." I didn't see who hissed the word "boy" like it was a crime. I scraped my blue suede boots against the bleachers until I was the last girl picked, shuffling over to my complaining teammates. There's no dialogue here because I never spoke back. I can tell you what the shoes looked like though, their thin suede that was no defense against angry foot stomps: bright blue patches, but mostly gray and flattened, soaked by the icy puddles of Detroit sidewalks. I spent too much time looking at my feet. The slick soles slid across the gym floor— I remember that the popular kids, Black, White and "Mixed," got picked first in some sort of complicated pecking order, while I tried not to let anyone know that I did care what they thought, praying that I didn't get chosen last.

We were almost that family, the lowest rung of White scraping along in the rich neighborhood, hoping some of that American Dream would rub off on us. We weren't as poor as the White family that had no furniture. Not as bad as the White family who didn't have enough food. But almost. The rich White kids were the most cutting, the most vicious. The Black kids were off in their own solar system, going to debutante balls and hanging out with the others whose parents played in the Detroit Symphony Orchestra, worked at the medical center, or recorded on the Motown label. I'd have given anything to be part of either group. If I'd been brave enough, maybe I would have joined forces with the other pale, freckled kids from Appalachia, but I didn't want to draw attention to myself. I counted on Jesus to save me.

When I finally graduated and made it into Cass Technical High School in downtown Detroit, a White girl I met at swim practice invited me to her home. I couldn't believe Lainey wanted to be my friend. Most White kids I had known were richer than we were and snobby. She was a White girl who was not at private school, talked with a Southern drawl, and thought my family was rich. When I was at her house in Southwest Detroit, I felt at home, as if I lived there already. I expected to see my doppelganger, wearing a pair of old Levi's, white high-tops, and a flannel shirt walking up to one of the other red shingle duplexes. I could imagine my parents, sipping a beer on the front porch, playing their instruments, and singing folk songs out in the open. If we lived over here, Mom wouldn't be taking in anyone's ironing just so we could stay in the big castle-like house in the University District, and I'd have school friends on my street.

Finding Lainey was like stepping backward through a threshold, then out again, and finding the world changed to one where I belonged. Kids played basketball in the middle of the street, weren't swallowed up inside their houses practicing the piano and studying. When I was little, I used to imagine a different world too. I put mountains and sunshine and clean skies in Detroit. Now I was more realistic. I wanted a place that would take me in and love me back.

When I took the bus after school past the Ambassador Bridge leading to Canada, past the oil refineries spewing their yellow smoke, to Lainey's house on the Southwest side, I felt both at home and drawn in by the undercurrent—people like us, people that looked me in the eye and nodded their heads. On the north side, Mom tried to fit in, but the church ladies didn't talk to us. They rejected my mother's offers of friendship, warm cookies, bread—all wasted labor. We never saw the inside of their homes. No invitations were extended to join the club of White. In those early days, we were also segregated along race, and I never even saw the inside of my Black friends' homes, nor they mine. My best friend, a Chicana girl, was forbidden by her doctor-father to come to our house. The isolation was terrible.

At home in our castle house, I'd think of any excuse to call Lainey, volunteer to scrub the pots from dinner, so I could tuck the black telephone under my chin and walk back and forth from the stove to the sink with the coiled phone cord swinging and getting tangled. My hands were immersed in the water, scrubbing at the glued-on onions on the bottom of the soup pot, my eyes drifting to the neighbor's back porch draped with flowers, the big, square brick house. Purple flowers, bright as dew, but no life, no people. Just a velvety quiet. I itched to get over to Lainey's street.

"So how's Beto? Did he call you?" Maybe some boy drama about Beto and his cute friend Jackson. I pictured Lainey on the other end of the line, sitting next to the window on the wobbly kitchen stool, peering down into the alley. Maybe "our boys" were hanging around the back picnic table at the Tastee-Freez, eating chili fries and sneaking cigs.

"Huh?" Lainey's voice came out slow, as if she couldn't pronounce consonants.

"Are Beto and Jackson around?"

Beto would sometimes go stand in the alley with Jackson and whistle if he thought Lainey's mom or her creepy boyfriend might be home and he didn't want to knock on the door. If Lainey thought Beto was in the vicinity, she'd develop a sudden craving for fries and make an excuse to go to the Tastee-Freez and promenade up and down Springwells to check out who's who, and who's wearing what, and who's with who. Oh, I wanted to be there, on the street where people came out of their houses and talked to each other.

"Soo?" I drew out the question.

"No, I don't know," Lainey said. "Raymond's been acting weird. He's been snorting coke since yesterday and keeps saying Mama is cheating on him."

I pictured her brown eyes wide and worried, her hair puffed out and tangled like it got when her mom's boyfriend started using too many drugs. She got too worried to even comb her hair or go to school. Crap.

"You'll be in school tomorrow, right?" I asked.

"'Course," she breathed. "I gotta go." She hung up quick.

I knew not to call back. I spent the rest of the evening staring at my world history book and taking notes, listening to my little sister bang on the piano and the hiss of the iron as Mom pressed the neighbor's laundry.

I didn't worry about Lainey until she missed morning swim practice. Cities were coming up, and she was our best diver. She should be at school. Maybe Lainey did sound strange the night before on the phone, but her mom's nasty boyfriend, Raymond, was scary. I decided to skip and make sure that Lainey and her little sister, Tammy, were okay. After morning practice, I hid in the locker room until the security guards, Bonnie and Clyde, cleared the hallways, then ran out the side door and walked downtown to the Baker bus stop. My friends were my life.

When I got to Senator Street, I could see that Lainey had been waiting for me, watching from the downstairs porch.

"Come up to my room."

We walked up with Tammy tagging along. Noises came from the bedrooms, whimpering. Lainey's mom and Raymond, I supposed, wrinkling my nose.

Lainey and I kept climbing, up to her attic room. We had painted it all black one day while listening to a Rolling Stones album. A double mattress lay under the front dormer window, behind a curtain and two old, ratty couches. Lainey and I climbed on the mattress, cracked the window, and lit up two Newport Lights.

"You guys shouldn't smoke," Tammy said.

"You should go to school," Lainey said, blowing a smoke ring in Tammy's face.

"You're sick." Tammy coughed. "I'm going to tell Mom."

Lainey rolled her eyes and handed Tammy a cigarette. "Just ask, you baby. Don't front." Lainey lifted the sheet tacked over the window and blew out a stream of smoke.

"We haven't slept all night," Lainey said. "Ray is completely wired." Their mom's boyfriend was crazy-acting without drugs, his big, bushy red beard and squinty blue eyes looking like a cross between Wile E. Coyote and a serial killer.

"Snorting coke?" I asked.

Lainey nodded. "I think so."

"Did you call Beto too?"

"Yeah, last night," Lainey said. "I told Beto if we didn't make it to school, it was because things were getting weird."

I frowned at Lainey, leaned out the window, and saw Jackson with his backward baseball cap and Beto's taller and bulkier form turn out of the alley and head toward the front porch. I waved my cigarette at them from the attic window, but Beto's head was turned toward Jackson.

Lainey leaned out the window. "Yo, Beto!"

Beto and Jackson turned and headed for the door.

"They shouldn't be up on the porch; don't they know Raymond is down there?" I asked. "Is his little girl down there too?"

"Yeah, Mom was watching Jamie. I think. Um. They shouldn't come. Yeah, yeah, tell them."

Oh crap. I smelled the weed on Lainey's hair. She was not thinking at all. I leaned out the window, trying to get the stupid boys to go away before they made things worse.

"Hey, Beto!" I shouted.

He climbed the porch stairs without glancing up.

"Jackson!" I waved, trying to get their attention.

The dogs started their barking chorus, and we heard Raymond's indistinct shouting. He hated people coming over. Oh shit. Especially someone like Lainey's friends.

We tried to shout again to tell the boys to go to the alley. Once Raymond's dogs were disturbed, there was no telling what Raymond would do. If they would just go away, we could figure out how to slip past Raymond, Lainey's mom, and little Jamie, and meet the boys in the back. Jackson should know better; his mother was always drinking. But the doorbell was already ringing, and the dogs started going crazy, running back and forth on the upstairs porch, lunging against the rails. The puppies in the side room yelped like babies.

We pounded down the attic stairs, hoping to get all the way to the front door first before Raymond did something stupid.

"What the fuck!" It was Raymond.

"Chill, Raymond, we'll get the door," Lainey said, but Raymond had already turned back to Lainey's mom.

"Who's at the door, Dinah?" he snarled. "One of your boyfriends?" He lurched toward her.

"Wait, Raymond!" Lainey put herself between Raymond and her mother. "I think it's our boys!"

Raymond tilted his head, looking at Lainey. "What, Dinah, you have your brat covering for you?" He shoved Lainey out of the way. "Little bitch," he added, reaching around Lainey and grabbing her mom by the hair. "Now why don't you tell me who your boyfriend is?" She twisted around, trying to relieve the pressure on her scalp.

Lainey and Tammy got between Raymond and their mom, until he released her.

"Fucking little bitches!" Raymond yelled, punching the wall. He let out a guttural sound somewhere between a growl and a shout. Then he reached behind the couch for something.

I lunged for the phone. He got there first, closed his big hands around the cord, and ripped it out of the wall. "Get the fuck out of my business!"

I hadn't seen what he'd grabbed from behind the couch until just then. He held his rifle up in his fist and shook it at us. "You girls, get in the kitchen now!"

The dogs were still going crazy, but the doorbell had stopped.

Raymond had me by the front of my flannel, his bleeding hand clenched into a fist. He shook me back and forth as he half-dragged me toward the back of the house. "You keep your fucking hands off the phone, little girl. You hear me? Don't you get cute and try to call the pigs on me."

The whites of his eyes had a pearly yellow film, spidery and bloodshot. Crude blue- and red-inked prison tattoos snaked up and down his muscled arms and circled his neck. A skeleton wearing a cowboy hat and a Confederate flag T-shirt stared at me before Raymond pushed his face up to mine. He shook me one more time. "Stay here," he growled, then let me go.

I heard his boots clomping down the hallway.

Out the kitchen window, I saw a flicker of movement down the alley, behind the Tastee-Freez. I heard sounds from everywhere: sirens, Raymond and Dinah screaming at each other in the other room. And yet, what I was staring at was the open jar of peanut butter on the counter. I felt ravenous and wanted to eat the whole jar.

Tammy, Lainey, and I stood in the kitchen, not knowing which way to go.

"Oh, god," Tammy said under her breath. Her freckles stood out in waxy relief from her pale face. She clutched my arm in panic.

"I think Jackson and them are out in the alley," I whispered to reassure her. "Maybe they already called 911." I hoped that Beto and Jackson would do something even better, call a fire truck or an ambulance, because they always came when you called. I hoped they would get help and not try some heroic rescue mission.

In the relative quiet, we heard another sound, one I realized had been there the whole time. "What's that noise?"

The sound came from the utility room where Raymond kept the breeding pups and his stash.

Tammy stuttered. "Jamie. It's Jamie!"

Was Raymond's three-year-old daughter trapped inside? Had she been there the whole time?

Then we heard the little Doberman pinscher puppies barking. And Jamie's cries turned into shrieks.

We ran to the room.

"Jamie. Honey. Open the door," I called.

She didn't stop wailing. Over the dogs barking, she couldn't hear me. I shook the door handle. It was locked, but the door was cheap.

"Jamie!" Tammy stuck her face near the keyhole. "Aunty Tammy is coming!"

The door was papery thin, and it started to come apart with a few quick kicks from our vinyl gym shoes. It shredded into long, splintered pieces.

I crawled halfway through and saw the puppies free from their cage. Jamie's face was pink and shiny, covered in saliva. I reached for Jamie's tiny red overalls, pulled her through the door, handed her to Tammy. She buried her face in her stepsister's neck.

"Raymond's in the living room with Mama," Lainey half-whispered, half-moaned. Even as she said this, we heard shouting and pounding on the front door. We had to get Jamie away from the dogs, out of the apartment.

"Get out! Go!" Tammy said, heading toward the back door with Jamie curled in her arms.

Lainey and I crept down the long dark hall toward the living room.

Raymond was shouting at whoever was pounding on the front door.

Then I heard shots from his rifle. "Hail Mary, full of grace, please help us," I prayed. I knew Jackson and Beto were crazy enough to try to help.

Across the hall was the linen closet with two wooden white doors and three drawers, just like the one at home. I wanted to crawl inside and come out in my own upstairs hallway. I felt my soul fly up and up, so high that Lainey and I were two pinpoints of light, seen from space. The roof of the house extended out toward the sky, and below stretched Senator Street with its bright tunnel of trees masking the soot-stained two-story house and the evil uncoiling inside. And we were just two girls huddled in shadows, in a darkened hallway.

"Holy Mary, pray for us sinners now," I said to myself.

I took two steps toward the closet, wrenched open the door and reached in for the iron. I knew it was going to be there. I liked its heft and weight. I imagined smashing it into Raymond's arm, making him drop his rifle.

"Can you hear Momma?" Lainey whispered. We waited for a long moment, straining to hear. We backed into the bathroom, shutting the door halfway.

At the front of the house, we heard a door smash open, then heavy footsteps up the stairs into the living room. A commotion of shouts and barking came from the porch, but no more shots.

"Let's go." I held the iron above my head like a torch. If I had to, I'd get him from the back, split his head in two.

Then we heard scuffling and "Don't touch me!"

We peeked around the corner. We didn't expect to see a paramedic sitting next to Lainey's mom on the couch. A light-skinned Black woman with short, curly hair held a compress to Dinah's head.

Lainey's mom was still wearing an apron from the bar, and she lifted it to wipe her mouth. "Fucking Christ. Who fucking called you people?" She winced in pain and twisted away from the paramedic. "The fuck?"

"Let go of me, you fucking pigs!" Raymond shouted in a coked frenzy, but three Detroit police officers had him pinned.

Lainey and I backed down the hallway as if avoiding broken glass. The kitchen clock showed it was 1:35 pm; I should have been in my tenth-grade honors English class, discussing the end of *The Lord of the Flies*.

I still had the iron in my hand. I set it on the yellow Formica table. "Your mom is fine, let's get out of here," I whispered to Lainey. Real grownups were in the house. Let them handle it, I thought.

Lainey and I melted down the back stairs and around the corner of the house to the side, where Tammy and little Jamie were huddled with Jackson and Beto. Tammy was gripping Beto's hand, leaning into him.

"Come on," I said. "Let's get away from the house."

We all joined a gathering crowd and stood together near the back. "It's fine," I said. "Your mom's okay." Tammy relaxed a little and shifted Jamie to her other arm, dropping Beto's hand.

"Man, you fucking White people are crazy," said Beto.

"Hombre, your dad sure loves his shit," added Jackson.

"He's not my dad," said Lainey.

"I'm not crazy," added Tammy.

On the street, two cops shoved Raymond into the back seat of the squad car.

"I guess I'm babysitting again," said Tammy, looking down at Jamie, then over at their mom, cursing at the cops.

"Motherfuckers! Where are you taking him?" She weaved behind the car as it pulled away, a cigarette dangling from her fat lip, and a black eye blooming, puffy, and red. "Damn it!" She pulled off her cracked heel and threw it at the cop car. It landed in the middle of the street, red and glittering.

I turned away so she wouldn't see me; she'd probably blame me for the ambulance and the police coming, but the number of neighbors who stood around smoking cigarettes and talking in little clumps shielded me from her evil eye. "Oh, girl, you should have slapped him!" one thin woman wearing an Aerosmith tank top said to Lainey's mom. Everyone laughed.

Tammy was replaying the entire scene to a rapt audience of other teens skipping school on a weekday afternoon, and I didn't think anyone would notice if I disappeared. Maybe I could make it back to school for French class, or even swim practice. It all had happened so fast, like heat lightning that flared up and then went away just as quickly, but when I lit a cigarette, my hand was shaking.

I headed to the bus stop on Springwells and looked down at my light blue student bus card—my escape ticket to downtown, to school, my passport home. My real home was in the castle house in the neighborhood that almost wasn't Detroit, where three of my sisters had already graduated from high school and moved on. I knew I would graduate too, just as I knew Raymond would be back. Lainey's mom would let him in again, maybe even that night, maybe the next day.

I leaned my head on the bus window. The autumn sunlight filtered through, casting a glow from another time and place, where attack dogs didn't lunge through the slats of upstairs porches, where translucent, blond-haired little girls didn't get locked in tiny hot bedrooms, where I wouldn't hear gunshots and wonder if someone I knew was lying at Raymond's feet.

Lunchtime at Cass Park

Elisa, 1981

"Hey girls. You want to party with us?"

I looked over to Tammy, and we exchanged glances.

"Uh, no thanks." She waited for me to answer them. "We were just eating lunch."

The men drew closer. One of them shoved a jar toward me. It looked like something in Mr. Krevnik's biology lab—scary. Maybe it was fingers preserved in blood instead of formaldehyde.

"Tamales, one dollar."

"Uh, no thanks." I pushed the jar back. It slipped and almost fell; my hands were slippery. I glanced over at Tammy. The sweat under her arms was blooming in a half-moon on her tight white satin halter.

The men had closed the half-circle around us, where we were sitting on the park bench. The tall one spoke again. He was wearing several layers of clothes, and they were permeated with the scent of piss, sweat, liquor—the perfume of hard living on the streets.

"We said," this time he raised his voice, menacing, his mouth twisted in a smile, "do you want to party with us?" A lighter flashed, and a moment later the familiar sweet smell of marijuana came from his joint, but also something else, acrid and unfamiliar.

We were only a block away from school, where we were supposed to be eating lunch in the cafeteria, and a block away from Detroit's theater district. But in this little park, an inviting patch of green that seemed like an oasis, we were miles away from help.

A tear melted Tammy's green eyeliner onto her face, forming a rivulet down her pinkened cheek. Tough Tammy? I took a deep breath, thinking fast. We were seated, and there were more of them than us in a half-circle around us. No quick escapes.

"Sure! But we have to get back for seventh period." I reached my hand out for the joint. I didn't want the slobber of every bum in Cass Park. I inhaled, but not deep. I could already tell it was strong. I tried to catch Tammy's eyes, but she missed my signal and inhaled deep. Shit. I'd probably have to drag her back to school. Tammy started giggling like a hyena, but I felt sick, like I had swallowed strychnine.

I lied. "Oh, man, that was some good shit." The men had relaxed, hanging out. "I have to get my friend to school, or her dad will kill her, but I'll be right back." I added this for insurance, just in case they weren't too stoned to start something.

"Come on, Tammy. Back to school. Now." I grabbed her by the elbow. "See you, guys." I aimed this at the group as we dragged off. The one with the red baseball cap with the oversized bill stared.

"See you," he repeated. I wasn't sure what I had just agreed to, but as I fought the urge to vomit into my French book, Mademoiselle Garas chirping, *"Sur le plage, dans l'eglise"* in a loud nasal staccato, I knew I'd never return to that park.

Meant to Disturb

Elisa, 1982

I should have been happy then. Picture a perfect past: I'm in honors English, and I'm on the Cass Tech swim team even though I am not a good swimmer. They let me race on the C team. I keep swimming into the other lanes and bumping the ropes. But still, I'm not bad. I'm in the orchestra too. But last night, Mom pulled a knife on me and said, "I could kill you, you know." She was cooking dinner, and she just showed the blade to me and pointed it at my chest, still bloody from trying to saw the meat up for a soup to stretch it for the eight of us. There's no way to take this thought, "My mother wishes I was dead," and turn it into anything bright and shiny. Part of me was turning into stone, but the other part has taken to sawing at my arm with my penknife.

I was telling you this story, but I want to tell you that it's thirty years later now, and Rebecca, who actually did lend me a car once, is dead, and Lainey is gone. Jackson was in jail for drugs, and Joaquin married Spooky and works for the gas company. I wrote Joaquin into this story, but you should know—I'm making that shit up. He spoke to me at swim team meets and soccer games. Joaquin signed my birthday card, but he stopped talking to us after we got him arrested. My parents didn't check on me, so I just took the bus all over Detroit, skipping school half the time.

The Mexican kids weren't really our friends. Something in them was always curling away from us in disgust because we, the White girls, were the dangerous ones. Me and Lainey and Rebecca.

But I'll tell you the story. Just read it, and pretend you are watching another Hollywood "urban" movie where the White kids are the saviors and the Brown kids barely have a speaking role. Then take the Mexicans out and put them back into their clean houses filled with cooking dinners. Set the Black kids down at their piano lessons, and when they get home, watch their dad, the school principal, make them do their homework. Now watch the trashy White kids high on something, with nobody looking at them with a camera and making it romantic. Watch the White kids on the sidewalk, after curfew, smoking cigarettes and eating chips for dinner.

Let me take you back to the past, where I'll tell you a fake story that makes me sound tough, romantic, and just a little crazy, but it's a lie. I'm telling you it's a lie. I was just all crazy, like all White people doing messed-up shit with nothing to lose and no one waiting with a siren, handcuffs, a police car, a grave.

I'm back in the past again. See? I'm in control, and I am going to show you my life like it's better than it is. I sound tough. See, Bitch? I'm from Detroit. So don't *fuck* with *me*! Are you scared? I'm making it up 'cause I'm a liar. I read that on a T-shirt. Ha ha. Welcome to Detroit, Now Get the Fuck Out.

Anyways, back in the past: I'm time traveling again. But I'm not crazy.

Tonight I'm sitting on Lainey's front porch on Senator Street, Southwest side, two miles from the Detroit River and the Ambassador Bridge to Canada, and 93 million miles away from the nearest star. Lainey, Rebecca, and I all have the idea of carving our boyfriends' initials on our arms. It's probably Rebecca's idea, but I already know that somehow I'm going to make it seem like mine. I do this a lot. Fucking Rebecca will say something stupid like, "Let's see if the school is open." But I'll be the one who breaks the locker room window and starts trying to flush the volleyballs down the boys locker room toilets. And I never get caught. Fucking Rebecca just got off two weeks of punishment for bringing JR up to her attic when she thought her mom wasn't home. Stupid bitch. She's my best friend, but she can be so fucking stupid. She can be flat-out dangerous.

I take my knife—actually Joaquin gave it to me. It's not even a Swiss Army knife; it's just a penknife, black, with ridges and a little silver oval nameplate I polish with the tail of my flannel shirt. I'm working on the "J," but it's not going well. When we started cutting the boys' initials on our arms, we were just going to make tiny tattoos so we'd all have them.

But I get a little jolt when I make the one clean line for the "J." As I slice into the skin, the pain moves all the way up my arm like an electric charge. I watch the blood seep up in a line, like a seam ripping open. The fresh jolt feels hot and sharp—even better than straight liquor. I'm floating, and everything seems laughable. I laugh out loud. I hear Rebecca, Lainey, and now Joaquin laughing too. But then I get to the curve of the "J," and I just can't make a clean cut. I take a sip of the horrible ouzo Rebecca stole from her parents, and a "V" of birds flies overhead, black construction paper cutouts, fleeing shadows. I want to follow them.

I look at my handiwork, and my knife moves of its own accord, digging into my arm like it's scraping off a lamb sandwich from the Golden Fleece. We're just meat, I think. A flap of skin moves aside, and a red bloom bubbles up.

"Elisa! What the fuck!" Rebecca shouts, but I wave her off and sit back on the concrete steps. I've broken through the dull buzz of the ouzo and the mellow high of Benny and Abel's best primo hash. Cutting is a high that sends me somewhere else entirely, and I am glad to be gone. I smell flowers, and I try to go into the flower cave and talk to Dad. But all I can see is a long, dark hallway, and I run as fast as I can and slip through to the other side. Everything is clear. At the end of the hallway is a stage, burnished, light-colored oak, lit with soft rose footlights. I can't see the audience, but I can sense them, hushed and waiting. They're here to see me. I'm not wearing my flannel and jeans anymore, but a dress, pewter gray–blue, low cut, no surgery scars now. It's me. I lift my arms. Maybe I'm going to conduct an orchestra. Maybe I'm about to find out something important. But I hear something. It's Mom, in the corner of the stage. "You. Are. Not. Allowed. Out. Get. Back. In. The. Kitchen." She speaks like some weird marionette. Then her voice changes, her face contorts. "You fucking bitch."

I know I'm in a fantasy, but here I've got the knife, and I decide who calls me bitch. Fucking mother, I can't even get a buzz without her dragging her ass into the corner of it.

"Goddamn it, Elisa!" Rebecca is screaming. "Come out of it! Joaquin, give this crazy bitch your bandana!"

I feel pressure on my arm, and I see Joaquin's thumb holding down his bandana. Blood's seeping through it, but I'm no longer in that other place. I push Rebecca back and shake off Joaquin's arm.

"I'm fine."

Lainey is smoking a joint, but Rebecca looks worried.

"Here. Let me look at that." I see a look of doubt in Joaquin's eyes.

I shrug and pull my knife out again. "Relax, you guys. See? Easy." I slice down once, deep, and the "J" is complete. The "H" is easy, three quick cuts, and a pair of perfect letters paints themselves on my skin. J.H. Joaquin Hernandez. I raise my eyebrows and signal Joaquin to tie the bandana on my arm. "We all agreed to give ourselves tattoos, and now you're all freaking out about nothing." I wipe the blade off on the bandanna and flip it closed. Rebecca and Lainey have their knives out too, but their mini tattoos barely need band-aids. Little pussies.

"Crazy bitch." Joaquin bends over and kisses me.

His mouth moves over mine, and I feel his lips, hot and insistent, but I'm not feeling it. I've been holding back; I realize I can be in two places at once. I'm seeing the red lines blooming on my arm, and I'm walking down the empty stage again. Mother is locked behind a gunmetal gray door this time. The stage is empty, clean. Just me present. I can be in this place, and nobody needs to know it.

My lips move in response to Joaquin. It's automatic, but I don't want him opening his eyes and seeing I'm not there again, so I lean into him and open my mouth a little wider, letting him deepen the kiss.

"Damn girl." Joaquin's eyes are hooded; I can tell he's excited. Rebecca laughs and waves her cigarette like a wand, magically producing a set of keys, which she tosses to Joaquin.

"Don't smoke in my dad's car!" She sidelong glances at me, and she's smiling so wide I can see her gold tooth. "I guess he likes your tattoo," she whispers. And then louder. "Go on, you two." She dismisses us with a wave and turns back to Lainey.

"Come on, girl." I let Joaquin pull me up, and I don't pull away when he slips his hand into my back pocket and squeezes. He peers around into my face. "Do I have the right girl?" he jokes and smooths the hair out of my eyes. We're by the car now and away from Lainey's porch that's a few houses down the street. I slowly turn my body toward him. I take his other hand and guide it to my other back pocket. When he squeezes again, I let myself completely press into him. I can feel his heat. I look directly at him.

"Oh, it's definitely me." I drop my eyes a fraction and see his Adam's apple move up and down in a gulp.

He takes the last two steps to the car in record time and wrenches the door open for me. I'm barely in before he's slamming the door and nearly sprinting to the driver's side.

We turn left on Vernor Avenue, so I know we're headed toward the parking lot by the closed rec center. It's almost all the way dark now; the smokestacks at the River Rouge Ford Plant are fading into the night sky. I can't think of a single reason to tell Joaquin to turn the car around and take me home. He puts his hand on my thigh, and I slide over and lean my head on his shoulder. I watch the blur of the neon signs and streetlights flashing by at a strange angle like the tail of a shooting star, headed for its new life.

Oh, yeah, that story is a complete lie, so you can turn off the ending credits and the sappy song. Here is what really happened:

It was Lainey's idea. She carved Viktor Molnar's initials into her arm with a pin. It was invisible within a week. Rebecca put Stasio Tomaszewski's name in her arm, also with a pin; since he didn't know she existed, it was good it disappeared in a week too, just little scratches really. On my sixteenth birthday, I drank a bottle of vodka with Lainey, and I sawed at my arm. I made a JH tattoo for Jackson Hensall. Not Joaquin Hernandez. Joaquin is a dream. He's the fairy-tale ending that girls like me will never get. Joaquin Hernandez goes inside when the streetlights come on and does his homework. JH is blond-haired, blue-eyed Jackson, the boy who kissed me once on the rocks near Zug Island and told me his eighth-grade teacher told him he was crazy. Crazy like me. They told me I was crazy too, so I branded myself with him, the blood seeping through my bandana and onto the floor. Another fairy-tale ending. And I didn't feel so alone because then we lived happily ever after. I still have the scar on my arm. Do you want to see it?

Oh, part of that's a lie too, but I still have the tattoo. Jackson never asked me out, and I have to stop this now. I have to stop lying 'cause it's getting easier. Here's the last layer. Joaquin did give me the knife. He was trying to be a friend, so I could protect myself against my mom and some of the girls at school, but I can't seem to stop cutting. I only have about twelve inches of scars that you can see are self-inflicted. OK, fourteen if you count the cut on my wrist from sticking my hand into the dog's face and trying to punch it. OK, forty if you count the ones you can't see if I don't wear shorts. OK, fifty if you count the blisters from wearing that belt under my skirt so I would remember to suck my breath in. OK, sixty if you count the accidental burns on my hands. OK, seventy if you count working a job where I have to smile too much and tuck my bleeding fingernails out of sight. OK, here's the truth. I am Frankenstein's monster. They are cutting ME. SHE keeps cutting ME.

This is more than a scar. This is a belief, old as time. Old as bone. Old as a curse, carved in stone. Die, Elisa. I could KILL YOU, you know. But it's not her voice anymore. It's my voice. MY VOICE. Saying that.

Darling Frankie

Elisa and Frankie, 1984

Frances Ailene Sinnett was my first baby, but at four years old, I was not cut out for motherhood. No matter how many times I pinched her toes and told her to shut up, it never got her to stop crying.

"Elisa." Fiona was bleary-eyed, trying to get Tory to use a spoon and stop burying her face in the potatoes. "Leave the baby alone. She's getting a new tooth." But Frankie was still MY baby. Fiona was seven and in charge of food and baths when Mother laid on the couch with a rag over her face. My job was to sit with Frankie and keep her from eating our crayons or stabbing herself with a Tinker Toy.

Frankie was never a very obedient child, even as she survived her babyhood.

"Frankie, come outside," I'd say.

"NO!" she'd answer and burst into tears. She liked the great indoors.

Frankie played with Dawn dolls and Barbies. She got new clothes, not hand-me-downs, because she refused to wear my old Garanimal T-shirts and boy's jeans. Mother put her in dresses, bows ironed. I think by that time Mom stopped apologizing for not giving birth to boys.

"This one's a girl." Mom must have decided to dress her like a baby doll, the first one of us to ever get new clothes, store-bought even. We stared at this creature, receiving Mother's adoration.

"Mom, can we have bread and jam?" Tory asked. Mom sliced off a piece and put it on Frankie's plate. "Can we play tea party too?"

"If you put on a dress." Mother said.

Tory's arms were crossed and furious. We weren't going to change out of our jeans and put on scratchy dresses. Tory and I exchanged a glance. Her blue eyes glinted.

"Come on, let's go outside," she said as we banged out the dented tin door. I stopped and picked up my baseball mitt and followed her. We didn't know we were the lucky ones. We were as free as the boys on the street, outside from dawn to dusk, burnt by the sun, scraped-up and wild-haired.

Frankie bloomed under Mother's careful attention. Her hair, her face, her figure were miniatures of our big sister Fiona/other mother, minus the exhausted face from taking care of us. On Frankie it looked perfect—black curly hair, thick lips, and smooth skin. Fiona almost won Miss Irish Detroit with her looks, but when the emcee asked her, "What does *Erin go Bragh* mean?" Fiona froze. She wasn't thinking, "Ireland forever." She was thinking, "Why does he keep looking at my chest? I am wearing a bra."

Mom bought new dresses for Frankie—nothing homemade for her. I remember the bright blue dress. It was beautiful, scratchy polyester, white ruffles and tights, and Mary Janes, spit-shined. Frankie was in the kitchen with Mom again.

I banged in through the side door. Frankie sat at the small table, a miniature teacup and saucer in front of her, her feet swinging a foot above the ground.

"Elisa." Frankie had just lost her two front teeth. "Do you want to play with me?" Her missing teeth gave her a lisp, so my name came out spitty and sounding like "Eleetha."

I felt Mom's attention shift away from the counter where she was pounding a loaf of bread into submission. Mother came to stand beside me, partially blocking Frankie from my view.

"No, Frankie," I said and turned around quickly, but not before 1 saw her face crumple. Mom wheeled back to her pounding. I ran back outside, but Frankie never followed.

It wasn't until the last of our four older sisters, Tory, moved out and Mom started college to study nursing that Frankie and I became closer. At the public high school downtown, I tended to skip class and get in trouble, so when it came time for Frankie to start ninth grade, high school in Detroit wasn't an option. I transferred, and the two of us were enrolled in a private Catholic school in the suburbs.

Mom and Dad had slowed down on their hands-on parenting by then. Mom was taking pills from work that had other people's names on the labels, and Dad lived in the basement, working on computer programs for the police department and playing his banjo until two o'clock in the morning.

When there were eight of us living in that giant brick house in the University District, the house seemed full; we'd always be tripping over someone or someone's friend. But now it was full of ghosts. After she finished up her algebra homework, Frankie would wait for me at the top of the attic stairs, piled under a mound of stuffed animals and blankets, 'til I got home. Like any good parent does when her baby can't sleep, I'd help Frankie, sneaking up some hot chocolate or a beer from the kitchen. I was a visitor from another planet, coming home from work at the restaurant, crawling into bed with a drink and a flashlight.

"Hey, Frankie, I'm home." I scooched up to her and leaned on her legs waving something in front of her face like a paper fan, then hid it behind my back. "Guess what I have here?"

"What? Let me see." She snatched at me. She was going to freak.

"Tiiiickets..." I drew out the first syllable with a sing-song voice.

"What what?!" She bounced up and down on her knees. I flashed the beam of light on her face; her overbite made her look like a nocturnal rodent. Our parents had given up on orthodontia about halfway through my treatment, so Frankie and I both resembled chipmunks.

"Well, I don't know, maybe you won't want to go." I waved them over my head while she tried to grab them.

"Prince and the Revolution!" she screeched.

"Sshhhhhh, the whole neighborhood can hear you," I said.

We huddled over the tickets, caressing them. I popped the top off one of Dad's Molson Canadians with my lighter, and we passed the bottle back and forth. Comforted by this, mother's milk. We drifted into sleep, like twins in the womb, warm at last.

The night of the concert was a school night, but we had tickets for the inaugural Prince and the Revolution *Purple Rain* show at Joe Louis Arena in downtown Detroit. It was going to be so hip!

I knew girls dressed up for these concerts, but I always dressed like I was ready for the barn with Levi's and a flannel. Frankie looked ready for Halloween with her Catholic school uniform skirt hiked up and paired with a white blouse and a school tie. She found a red vinyl jacket from the attic and wore one glove. I didn't have the heart to tell her we were going to see Prince, not Michael Jackson, so instead I said, "Come on, Frankie, you look great."

I grabbed one of Dad's old jackets, army green with multiple pockets. I'd been siphoning off Dad's whiskey, a little bit each night, and now we had a Velvet peanut butter jar full.

We drove down Muirland Street and its tunnel of trees past 6 Mile, past 5 Mile, to the Lodge freeway and rolled downtown to the Joe Louis Arena. It was the new hockey stadium, right on the Detroit River, facing Windsor, Ontario, like a giant gray-and-white wedding cake. I handed Frankie the jar.

"This one is going to be tough to sneak in." Frankie took a swig and didn't sputter. She lit a few cigarettes. I sipped on the whiskey and smoked. I'd been driving since I was twelve, so going downtown in the Buick Skylark, even under the influence of a little whiskey, was no big deal. We needed to be properl y buzzed. I parked the car on Fort Street by the Presbyterian Church, and we walked downtown, passing the jar back and forth until I slipped it into the pocket of the oversized coat when we got closer to the arena. Our tickets were on the main floor, way in the back. We stood. Frankie looked around at the other girls and hiked her skirt up more.

"Elisa, give me a comb." I reached for the one in my back pocket and combed my feathered hair, then handed it to her. She took off her school tie and teased her hair so it puffed up.

"Frankie, you look like Apolonia Six!" I couldn't believe how she had changed her look in a matter of seconds. I took a deep drink of whiskey and looked back at her. The Michael Jackson jacket and glove were nowhere in sight.

By the time Prince came to the stage in his royal hues, we were truly wasted and sang and danced along to every song. In the back of the main floor, nobody cared if we sang along, smoked, or drank. When the purple light pointed at the audience, we screamed, a purple haze of smoke above our heads. "I think I looooovvve you!" we sang.

Then came the song "Darling Nikki." Giant beds were lifted, and a dancer wearing nothing but a cami and panties thrust and twisted on the bed. Should I cover Frankie's eyes? She was still in tenth grade! She slapped my hand away. Frankie undid two buttons of her blouse and began to dance in a way that was *nothing* like the Irish dancing we did down at the Gaelic League. Frankie raised her hands above her head, moving her hands in a back-and-forth twisting motion. It was as if my baby sister had become Darling Nikki. I didn't have the heart to stop her. I couldn't be like her, like an awakened genie, so I took another swig of whiskey and passed the jar to Frankie. I shouted and danced and threw Dad's coat down on a seat and didn't care if I ever saw it again. I would never be sensual and beautiful like Frankie, but I could be a good sport.

The whiskey buzz was making a retreat, and I could taste my mouth, sour and smoky. Prince was singing his encore, "I Would

Die for You." Everyone in the audience did the motions and sang along with him, pretending to shoot themselves in the head for Prince. Maybe he was the devil! I was shaking. Jesus died for us, but would we die for Prince? I stopped doing the motions and whispered to Frankie.

"STOP it, that's demonic." She knew what I was talking about. She stopped too, frightened of what we'd been doing.

I grabbed Dad's coat as we left the concert early, ducking out. We didn't promise our fealty to Prince, but Darling Frankie was born. I made her button her shirt, even though Mom and Dad were rarely awake to greet us. We pulled into our neighborhood, past the quiet blocks of large brick houses, and into the driveway. We slipped into the tiled foyer with its stained-glass doorway and past Dad snoring on the couch. We crept up to our room and finished the rest of the whiskey and whispered in the dark until we fell asleep.

In the morning I woke up to the sound of paper ripping. Frankie was ripping pictures of unicorns and rainbows from the wall as she stood on the bed. Sinking into the mattress, springs creaking as she walked back and forth, Frankie peeled tape and stuck it to the thick plaster wall. She picked up a stack of pages and began hanging them up in an arc. Her own drawings mixed with cut-out textile squares from *National Geographic* and pictures from magazines like *Vogue* we picked from the neighbor's recycle bundles. One pictured a young woman with a short and stylish haircut wearing a bright pink jacket, waving a scarf in the sky above her head, the sky a deep blue. Her face pointed up, and she was smiling.

"What do you think, Elisa?" Frankie was still trying to untangle her long hair.

"I think that haircut would look great on you, FrannyBanana." I climbed out of bed and started digging around on the floor for something to wear to school.

"It's Frankie. Call me Darling Frankie."

By Thanksgiving two weeks later, Darling Frankie had thrown the house into an uproar, cut her hair except for a long purple tail, and started her fashion merchandising career by altering her

Catholic school uniform into a miniskirt. This was blamed on me, of course, Mom sputtering and spewing.

"What kind of influence are you on your sister? This has got to be your fault. Do you know how expensive those wool skirts are? She can't go to school like that!"

"All right, Mom." I managed to squeeze by her.

"The timer is going off." She hurried back to the kitchen.

Then Frankie whispered to me about her new boyfriend.

"Jordan Lee? Are you serious? He's gorgeous!"

"Ssshhh! Don't tell Mom." Jordan Lee was off limits. Not only was he from the other side of 7 Mile (read: Palmer Woods; read: rich), he was Black, and Mom didn't want us dating Black boys, claiming, "You wouldn't be able to handle the pressure."

"Like she cares," said Frankie. "It's our business. We're in love." I looked at Frankie with her Algebra II book. Maybe she could handle it; she proved she could handle algebra.

"Well, if it doesn't work out, there's always Jaylen." Jordan had a twin, possibly even cuter than him.

Frankie laughed. "And I'm telling Mom I'm not going to college. I'm going to be an artist."

I didn't know what had gotten into her, but I liked it. I worried she wouldn't be able to keep up, sitting home alone or filling her time with Jordan Lee when I went away to the Army ROTC and college. But I liked the way she was filling up her wall with art.

"Elisa, let's go for a walk." She started winding a scarf around her neck. I put on my coat.

"Come on, let's go."

We went outside and started walking towards 6 Mile, toward the playground at Gesu. It was getting dark already. November's skeletal trees rattled, and the air promised snow. Gesu Church and school loomed ahead.

"I can't believe we used to be such little kids," Frankie said. "I'm not little anymore. I'm going to tell Mom."

"You're going to tell her what?"

"About me and Jordan. I'm getting tired of sneaking around," Frankie said. She looked so serious. I couldn't believe this was my baby sister. She wore a wool coat tied with a brocaded tassel belt. It looked like the curtain pull that had been missing from the library curtains, but on her it looked amazing.

"Frankie, do not tell anything that Mom will use against you," I answered, afraid for her.

"Oh, Elisa, my grades are up. Mom will be happy. And besides, it's going to be Christmas."

She had a point. The snow sparkled in the light of the streetlamp.

"We better get back." We hurried away from our childhood, running through snow and shadows toward home. The future was bright.

The Lives of Girls and Boys:
The 1960s–1970s

What They Were Told

Mother's Milk

Violet

The Writer

Dinnertime

Merry Christmas, Baby Jesus

Love Smells like Alcohol and Looks like Jesus

One of Those Girls

What They Were Told

Elisa, 1967

I felt it before I was born, felt my father's pulsing prayer.

"Not another girl, not another girl, please, Jesus, not another girl."

I tried to rearrange myself in the womb; acrid blood filling every open spot—nose, mouth, ears. I was not an easy sleeper down there, so I heard everything. I grabbed at my heart for a piece of flesh to mold into a baby boy's body. My fist struck something floating beside me, smaller, shriveling, my twin brother. He never made the light of day, and me, I never finished building myself into the boy my father wanted so he could show the world what a man he was, stop being bullied. I couldn't be the boy my mother wanted either so I would be the last. But I, baby number five, was not only not a boy, but also the worst kind of girl—a girl who had just one breast, no major pectoralis muscle, a sternum poking up through my chest like another alien baby was going to be born, but all in all, another girl.

My existence meant another mouth to feed, bottle full of milk flakes propped in the corner on a frayed blanket, while a bustling room full of girls, girls, girls in diapers drooled, tried out the potty chair, pulled down the curtains, begged for more potato flakes and pears from the backyard alley tree, circled my mother like tiny vultures.

Mother and Dad worried about how much money a deformed alien baby would cost. When I needed to be seen by the doctor, they waited a month for the appointment and took me all the way downtown. They had to leave my sisters with the elderly Mrs. Miller, regardless of her inability to keep them from running outside and flapping out into the middle of Stansbury Street.

It was the Summer of Love, and in San Francisco the children of the wealthy wore bell bottoms and smoked weed, but in Detroit people rioted, and tanks rumbled down the street. My parents, oblivious to current events, even as they were being televised and broadcast to the whole nation, were in their own private purgatory. They wove past a man and his son handing new shoes through a shattered plate glass window to a group standing on the sidewalk. Tense and worried, they stepped around the crowd. They wanted to get back to our house on Stansbury Street in case Mrs. Miller had lost one of my sisters or the uprising had reached our street. They parked the Mercury on a side street near the medical center and carried me the two blocks to the appointment.

They waited, thumbing through an old *National Geographic*. On the grainy black-and-white television set, coverage of the escalating violence and the National Guard converging on Detroit crackled and faded out. Maybe they didn't have to wait long; maybe the doctor didn't look at my mother's do-it-yourself haircut and Dad's taped-up horned rims and instead talked to them very slowly. Maybe he was going to tell them that I would be all right.

"There's something wrong with the baby, look at her, there's a hole in her chest." Mother thrust me into the doctor's reluctant arms. "What's wrong with the baby?" she implored.

He set me down on the examining table, the cold metal feeling like a punishment. A few minutes later he said, "This baby has a birth defect. It's not a hole. It's called Poland syndrome; she's missing the muscle there." He pushed me back into my father's arms; Mom's arms were crossed, staring at the doctor. "I'm sorry. She'll always be weak, always have trouble. But there's nothing that can be done about it."

Elsewhere in the city, a few miles away, tanks were advancing on unarmed civilians, but here at the medical center, Mom didn't take me from Dad's arms. She didn't want a baby who needed too much. Dad held me. Maybe he worried about me and my weak chest, angry and scared, wondering how he was going to make the house payment, but he didn't let go. Mother placed her gloved hand in the crook of Dad's elbow, and they walked without speaking, past the crowds, all the way to the car. At least, that's the way I imagined it. Maybe there was a moment that Mother held me and defended me, parted the seas, loved me the most.

Mother's Milk

Marie, 1969

It's morning. I've laid next to that randy goat of a husband for far too long, and this castle house is just another prison. I wear my white nightgown, it's worn thin with the passage of time and six girl babies, one after the other tugging, pulling on me. We live in the swanky area of Detroit where there are three-story brick houses with maid's quarters. No maids here, just the randy goat's old mother who doesn't know when it's time to go home and more fucking kids in every possible corner of the house. It's me taking in the neighbor's laundry, ironing, anything to stay in the house in mansion land with the Catholic school down by 6 Mile.

This bathroom window is ridiculously placed in the center turret of our castle house, but it's just a Rapunzel tower with a toilet. Like kids getting dressed up for Halloween, these houses are all pretending to be royal, but our family, the hillbillies of Detroit, are here instead. I get the kids as clean as I can before I send them outside to play, but their hair is thick and curly and impossible to comb, their freckled little faces are always dirty and sunburned, and the neighbors don't invite me to their afternoon card parties. I lean out of the bathroom window, my legs still sticky from the man goat. I'll have to do laundry again.

I lean out farther. Would it kill me instantly if I fell? Is there anybody who would care? Come to see me? No. They won't come where the Black people live. Maybe that's a good thing. Black people. I never saw one growing up. Not a Jew either. Mother warned me about them. In high school the few Black kids stuck to themselves; didn't bother me. Now they are here, next door, and in the neighborhood across 7 Mile, where the streets are curvy and the houses have tennis courts and circular driveways. In Detroit, Black people are the teachers and the doctors and the judges, but Mother still won't come.

I should just let myself fall, my nightgown spread out like an angel's wings, and I'll fly. The trees are glittering in the sun now, and Dr. Jackson is playing his harp with the window open next door. What if I took the kids' handcuffs from their cops and robbers set? I wouldn't be able to break my fall if I couldn't get my hands out. I would just land on my fucking head.

"Good morning, Marie." It's Mrs. Feinstone, the Jewish lady, pushing a stroller down the street. "Want to walk?"

The one person on the block who will actually talk to me, and she does her own laundry, refuses to take a maid. I step back quickly, stepping on the sharp corner of the screen, back into the house. Probably would just break my arm and not my head anyway, and still have to do it all with one arm. And how to explain it to the neighbors? At church? Landing on the concrete porch wearing part of a kids play cops and robbers set?

"Mommy?" It's Fiona. The girl who never knocks, carrying the baby. "She's stinky, Mommy." She doesn't even glance at the window.

"You know where the diapers are. Give her a bath." There are other bathrooms in this mausoleum. Three bathtubs to scrub. Three bathrooms with tiny white or faded pink or pale yellow tiles that show every speck and fleck of urine, toothpaste, soap scum, blood. And two more half-baths with toilets, so all of my children, except for the one that will be shitting in her diaper, could all be sitting on toilets at the same time and peeing and not wiping properly, making a fucking mess for me to clean, not like the neighbors who have maids in their maid's quarters and not the randy goat's mother here for a visit that never ends.

"Mama?" It's not Fiona. She's already gone to clean the baby. It's Elisa. Always trailing and sneaking behind one of the others who are useful and have something to say, news to bring, mail to show, boiling water to report, the oven timer reeling off, or the rain starting and the wash needing to come in.

Not this one. She's three. Almost four. She doesn't ask for anything. She stands there in judgment and looks at the open window, the screen pulled off, the place on my nightgown with the blood I wiped off my hand. I didn't know until just then that my hands are bleeding.

"Mama?" She tries to meet my eyes. I see fear, a questioning, something else. She steps toward me, arms opening for a hug. Wanting, wanting, always wanting something. Judging me and wanting more, always more.

"What do you want?" I ignore her outstretched arms. "Go on, go get dressed. Help your sister with the baby."

I pick up the closest thing to me, a hairbrush, and point it at her, make sure she looks right at me, gets the message. Her hair is shiny and black, tangled, her face square and freckled. Every inch of her squirming baby-fresh skin has extracted a price from me, and she doesn't even look like me. She's all her father's child, everyone's little darling. I can see the purple spider veins creeping across my legs; this is what blooms on me.

"GO!" I move toward her, a sudden lunge. She gets the message now, turns and runs.

I better wash up and get dressed before the randy goat comes in here, looking for number seven, trying again for a boy. Sometimes I remember the feeling of one of the babies' heads resting on my chest, the sweet smell of milk on her breath. But there's so many of them now, grasping, wanting. Maybe I'm losing my mind—it's been so long since I've slept the night through.

I turn the water on until it's scalding me and scrub and scrub until the skin is raw and pink. The pain feels good. Time for morning to start. I sit down in front of the mirrored vanity and pick up a tube of lipstick to paint on a smile. Time to be Mom.

Violet

Elisa, 1973

There's a cool, cool cave in our backyard. It's not made of rocks or sticks. It's made of flowers. They have names, but I don't know them. I can't remember things like that. The bright yellow flowers on a stick come first. Then the light purple ones that smell so good and grow in cones. And then the white umbrellas that the ants like to live in. On the ground making a fairy ring around my cave of flowers are the violets. Grandma taught me this name. I can remember things from Grandma. She doesn't yell, and violets are her favorite. They are dark purple or almost blue or dark purple and white. Violet is another name for their color. My name is Violet when I play under the flower bushes. Dad calls me Violet when nobody can hear him. But mostly people scream my name "ELISA ELISA!" They say I don't listen.

There is a secret hole in the fence, and when I go through it, I come out in the same back yard. It's a mirror world. Exactly the same and exactly the opposite. I run through the back yard and find I can do cartwheels and handstands. My arms are the same length in the mirror world. I'm going to run to the playground and see if the mirror world will let me hang on the monkey bars. I stop in front of the house, and here come my older sisters down the steps—TeresaFionaDarcyTory—always one year and one grade apart. It must be a school day in mirror land. We are all wearing plaid jumpers that say Gesu.

"Hi, Elisa," Fiona says. She wants to catch up with Stacey Pawloski and her little brother, Paul, so we run. Fiona is fast, but I am faster. Paul has turned into his dog, Lacey, so I turn into Domino, and we run ahead of Stacey and Fiona. Barking and chasing squirrels. We make it to the lower elementary doors by ourselves and turn back into ourselves, just in time to get marched inside by Sister Diane. I'm not sitting in the retarded kid chair in math class anymore. Sister Diane lets me write the answer down without showing my work. She just looks at my paper and smiles, doesn't grab me, moves onto the next question.

Our school is beautiful. It looks like it should live in pictures of New Mexico in the World Book Encyclopedia. It is made of thick white stone and has a red tile roof. But it looks out on a busy street, 6 Mile, because we are six miles from the Detroit River and Canada. Our class lines up and goes to gym class, and I take my usual place by the window. I can see that 6 Mile has disappeared. I can see mountains and pine trees.

"Elisa." I hear my name the first time someone says it. Sister Rosalind has a whistle around her neck. She speaks kindly.

"It's your turn on the ropes before we go to the playground." I follow my gym teacher to the mats and see the knotted rope going all the way up to the ceiling. I've never made it to the second knot, but we are in mirror land and I think I'm going to get to the top. I start to make the sign of the cross, and my hand stops above my heart. My chest is flat, no bone peeking out. I stretch my arms, and they are still the same length. I climb up, up, up to the top. Joanna Temple and Katie Chapman's mouths are gaping like my pet goldfish waiting for food, but they are not laughing. Sister Rosalind blows her whistle, and I float back down. I climbed higher than all of the boys. I'm at the front of the line today, and nobody slams the playground gate in my face. The others let me on the merry-go-round. They give me a turn on the swings, and I swing up, up, up to the sky, and then I see him. It's a Canadian Husky dog. He looks a little worn, like the heat of Detroit is too much for his thick hair. There are scratch marks across his face. Deep marks from fingernails.

"It's time to go back, Violet," he barks.

"Do we have to?" I ask, climbing off the swing.

"It's time." He always brings me back. I turn into Domino again, and we trot through the mirror streets past the big stone houses and through the mirror yard and back through the mirror. Flowers. I am alone in the flower cave. There is a humming in the air. A symphony of insects, Grandma told me.

"Violet." It's Dad. Standing outside the fairy ring, saying only my otherworld name. He is the only one in my family who knows it.

"It's time for dinner." He holds the branches aside for me to crawl out.

"Elisa, Denny, come to the table." Mom is waiting.

"It's time to wash up," Dad says. He puts out his arms, and I jump in and take a ride to the house.

The Writer

Elisa, 1977

I tried out different phrases like "knife edge of hunger," and I wrote lists of words for my story brainstorm: gnawing, mealy, glare, barren, growling, anxious, but I couldn't finish my language arts assignment for my sixth-grade English class. Mrs. Collins wrote in red pen:

"Your images are cliché; you can't possibly know anything about hunger, living in the neighborhood you do."

I muttered to myself as if I were in a confessional booth. "I shall not write about things I know nothing about. I will avoid clichés."

Mrs. Collins gesticulated to the class, then folded her palms together, pleading. "Write about things you and your classmates know." Francisca leaned over, poked me, and pointed at the margins of her notebook. She'd drawn Mrs. Collins with the body of a horse and a neighing head. I put my head down. Francisca made neighing sounds under her breath, just loud enough for me to hear. I forced myself to start coughing.

"Girls, settle down," Mrs. Collins scolded. "Begin your rewrites."

I started the list again with words I thought Mrs. Collins would like. Golf club, velvet, bridge club, automobile, cleaned, ironed, vacuumed, washed. I imagined stupid Katie Chapman wrote about people living in clean houses. Katie Chapman had a maid, so probably the maid washed and ironed Katie Chapman's school uniforms. That was the kind of thing Mrs. Collins liked to see, a proper story.

I showed Francisca the first story about me, the White girl who eats watery oatmeal every day for breakfast. Then the girl goes to school and sits with her best friend and draws pictures of the teacher. After choir class she forgets her blue cardigan sweater, so she goes backstage and sees the boy she has a crush on kiss the other boy behind the velvet curtain. One of the boys is crying. She picks up the sweater and backs away. Her stomach grumbles, and they both look up as if a string has jerked their heads like puppets, but she backs away. She is crying too. The nicest boy in her class, the only one who speaks to her, is kissing another boy.

I knew better than to include that in my story, but I kept the phrase about love and velvet curtains. Francisca gave me a thumbs-up and leaned in to talk or draw another cartoon, but Mrs. Collins loomed behind, peering at my page.

"Don't copy sentences from cheap magazines."

Francisca rolled her eyes, and I started to crumple it up, but Francisca glared at me until I tucked the first story in my denim bag made of jean shorts. I started to write another story, using the words I thought Mrs. Collins would approve. I wrote a story about a Black woman whose first name was the same name as the Chapman's live-in help, Deidre. I wrote about Katie coming to school in her ironed uniform skirt. Then Katie's mom came home from the doctor and took a little white pill, and Mr. Chapman came home and drank a tall drink with the glass "sweating and glistening." I put a little red cherry and an olive on top of his drink. That made him sound like the kind of dad I was supposed to know about, not like my dad who made the amber liquid in the basement, then drank it out of a jelly jar.

I looked at my story. There was no story. No words like knife, velvet, despair, and thieves. I kept writing; something had to happen. So I added a carpet, no dog pee, rich and plush, furniture new and clean, heavy red cushions, like something stolen from a confessional booth, but the only confession worth telling was a secret. The maid was pregnant. Who was the father? So Mr. Chapman gave her a fat envelope, and then there were whispers, and Deidre never came back. I imagined her taking a bus to the university, taking a class, never working as a maid, never doing anyone's laundry again. Maybe Deidre came back with a brand-new car, a Ford, and ran over Mr. Chapman with it. No. She ran over Katie, the biggest bully of the sixth grade. That's what I wrote as the ending.

That's what I did imagine, and most of what I wrote was not true, except for the ending. I wanted to be the one driving the car and running over Katie Chapman, the meanest girl in the school. Francisca loved the story, especially the ending. But Mrs. Collins pulled me by the ear to the principal's office and left me in a chair to wait for Sister Stella to call my mother.

"You need a psychiatrist," Mrs. Collins said before turning and going back to class. I wished Mrs. Collins was a nun; they were easier. They'd smack you if they didn't like what you said. They didn't stand there like bats with flowery caftans flopping down and saying "Express yourselves. It's the age of Aquarius!" They didn't trick you and then drag you down to the principal's office for following their advice.

I stared down at my scuffed Buster Browns, then back at the door of the principal's office. I squirmed in my chair and found a stray thread coming out of my navy blue sock and pulled on it, watching my sock unravel and become shorter and shorter.

My eyes drifted down the hall, counting the tiles until they landed on a familiar pair of shoes. "Francisca!"

Francisca made a "shhh" sign with her finger as she turned the corner toward the gymnasium.

Then I heard the breaking of the glass as the fire alarm sounded, loud and pulsing. I stood, looking to the right and the left, but then Francisca ran by.

"Come on," she called as she tugged at my arm and made for the stairs. I followed, hesitating only for a moment, then joined the river of students wearing the green-and-gray plaid. Our exodus was orderly at first under the watchful eyes of the nuns, fire trucks sounding in the distance. As we spilled out into the autumn sunshine, we multiplied and fanned out, raised our hands and ran, like a kaleidoscope of butterflies, catching an air current, flying to freedom.

Dinnertime

Teresa, Fiona, Darcy, Tory, Elisa, Frankie, 1970

My older sister Tory is standing at the table, eating her mashed potatoes without silverware, looking like a pig eating from a trough. We are all laughing. We don't remember what infraction Tory committed at the table, only that she's lost her chair and her silverware.

"Go! Go! Go!" Teresa (sister #1), Fiona (#2), Darcy (#3), Frankie (#6) (banging her spoon on her highchair), and I (#5) are cheering for Tory (#4) as she snorfles up her food.

Dinnertime is a merry affair, and even punishments take on a circus tone. Tory gets in trouble on purpose so we can have punishments, because it's fun not having to use silverware and watching little Frankie pound her spoon on her metal highchair tray. She's got a good sense of rhythm. I don't think Mom is mad.

This was before, when we all sat down together every night after watching *Lost in Space* and *Gilligan's Island* on the rabbit ear TV while one unlucky sister had to set the table and help with dinner. Dad quizzed us on math and spelling, and Mom taught us memory tricks and ladled out the mashed potatoes.

Most of the time we sat down together. We were eight. And it was very good.

Merry Christmas, Baby Jesus

Elisa and Teresa, 1981

My sister Teresa was the mother of Baby Jesus.

I bought him at a novelty gift kiosk at Northland Mall in a last-minute impulse buy. I was headed over to the Pied Piper party store to buy a fifth of Bacardi or a carton of Marlboros for Teresa. She was coming home for Christmas from Myrtle Beach, and I knew how she liked to party.

For my other four siblings, I stuck to the basement of Hudson's, where even bargain sweaters got wrapped in classy-looking dark green boxes.

My bags were heavy; my wages from serving dinner parties at Mrs. Rosenthal's and scrubbing down the chili pots at Wendy's were gone. I could already imagine my family opening the boxes, giving fake smiles, and kicking the gifts under the tree on the way to the refrigerator for another drink. The next day I'd stand outside the living room and watch them scramble around with their hangovers: "Whose ugly sweater is this?" and "Where's my fucking radio?"

Buying presents for Teresa was different. I didn't have to buy her stuff for a so-called "high achiever" headed for the Army or college and a real job. Teresa wasn't like that; she was about reality. I always tried to buy her three or four presents. One to make her laugh, some liquor or cigarettes, and something cool, like a picture of us in a new frame or a new hat box filled with stuff from the pharmacy that I knew she couldn't afford. She'd been living away from home on and off since she was about fifteen, and I always got her the best presents.

The baby was a gag gift, a giant, glossy cardboard doll on a base with Gerber Baby blue eyes and curly blond hair. I think it kind of looked like Teresa. Maybe this baby was welcomed—crawling across a nursery floor like in *Peter Pan* in a blue nightgown and a dog as a nanny. Mom was always telling Teresa, "Don't get pregnant. You should never have a baby." So I bought her one.

Getting her liquor and cigarettes took a little longer. Sometimes I could go right up to the bulletproof glass counter at the Sailor Time Party Store on 7 Mile and buy whatever I needed, mumbling that my dad needed something.

"My dad needs a carton of cigarettes," or "My dad needs a fifth of Bacardi." My dad drank and smoked a lot. If Mr. Hassan ever met my dad, of course he would discover that my dad didn't smoke, and he only drank whiskey. If his uncle was there, he'd glare at us in our short skirts and bare arms and ask us for our ID. Today was one of those days. I didn't even want to bother getting out of the car. Four of us shared the 1963 Dodge Dart. I learned how to drive the "three-on-the-tree" stick shift on that sweet red car when I was only fourteen, and I could drive anything, even a tractor up on our cousin's farm in Canada. Teresa received a used black Camaro when she turned nineteen because it was going to make her stop using cocaine. I didn't know if it had worked, but she still had the car. None of us used cocaine, but the next oldest, Fiona, got pretty crazy with weed, and no one offered her a car. Frankie, my baby sister, was still too young to drive, and I had my permit, but if the others were busy working, like today, I took the car. No problem. The police couldn't tell us apart anyway and we only drove the Dart up and down Livernois, up and down 7 Mile, 6 Mile, and sometimes the Lodge Freeway. That was it.

Mr. Hassan wasn't around, and there was only so long I could stand in the store looking at the beef jerky and the potato chips with his old uncle glaring at me, so I went back to the parking lot and headed down to the dreaded Pied Piper, down Livernois, almost to the Lodge. There I stood outside of the liquor store where White girls like me tended to get jumped because everyone in the neighborhood knew we had cash on us and were waiting for someone over twenty-one to go in the store and buy us some contraband. I waited around until I convinced a guy to go in and buy me a carton of smokes and a fifth of Bacardi for Teresa; the price was one pack of cigarettes and another half pint for the guy. I did the transaction and kept things straight, but the price could be even higher, depending on who I got to buy for me. And then I was all set with Teresa's Christmas present.

Christmas was a big deal around our house. Dad started building things in the basement around October. Last year he built us all desks from sheets of plywood, old doors, and giant wooden dowels. I loved my desk, even though it was a bit wobbly. This year he was making us mini speaker cabinets and covering the wood with contact paper. I heard him swearing, "Goddamn it." I peeked in at him, wrapping himself up like a mummy with mirrored contact paper. I knew it would be worse if I went in, so I kept going, pretty sure he would get unstuck by himself.

Mom had a terrible temper, especially when Teresa came home. Dad and Teresa fought every year—always something about money or drugs. But that'd be only one squall, and then the air would clear. We knew it would happen, and it wasn't like we were waiting for the moment for Teresa to start a fight with Dad; we just knew it was inevitable. Mom would melt down, and we would get drunk for about three days, except for Mom who'd be onto the pills she stole from the hospital. But it was still fun.

Mom knew every Christmas carol in the songbook, we knew the ones from the TV shows, and we sang. And of course we had the whole "Appalachian Christmas Favorites" set we pulled out every time the family band played a holiday gig, but we'd have to be really drunk to sing those. We made up verses and did our best to make the world's ugliest Christmas cookies so we didn't have to give any of them away. Mom was a killer baker, and her cookies were the best; the icing, after hardening for one day, was perfect. The three youngest of us had a plan. Tory, Frankie, and I put just enough red food coloring into the white icing so it looked like Pepto Bismol, the nastiest shade of pink known to man, and the color of the dog poison big, stupid Albert next door fed his dog.

After the Pepto pink icing, we added green and blue so they looked like a nasty purply-brown, almost like something you'd find in the bathroom after someone had been drinking too much and missed the toilet when they were puking. We iced all the cookies with that pink and brown icing and threw on some red and green granulated sugar. When Mom got home and saw them, she was going to hit us with the wooden spoon, and then she just started laughing. Oh *God*, you just never knew which Mom you were going to get.

Then Mom started cooking a giant pot of potatoes and a giant corned beef and cabbage and beer, and Christmas became our histories and our hopes all brining and boiling together. Mom didn't have Christmas when she was little, so we were all making up for it. Dad finally finished his carpentry project down in the basement, and then we sat around the fire and everyone over fifteen started drinking, which meant everyone over twelve. Everyone but Frankie and Mom was drinking and smoking weed sneakily up the fireplace. We all piled the presents except for Santa, who would bring about a hundred more. Mom wrapped up everything she had bought for us and hid for the past six months. And for some reason, she always wrapped up a can of salmon and a can of Spam for everyone. "You need protein."

After the wooden clock on the mantel struck midnight, we put out a bowl of milk for the reindeer and some crazy-looking cookies for Santa. We fell asleep listening to the rustling downstairs. If last year was typical, we'd get some homemade wooden stuff from Dad, a book from Mom that she made, and then everything on sale at the Hudson's basement and the Kresge sale table. Sweaters in a strange color, beauty items, a grocery bag of books from the second hand, stocking full of ribbon candy and Zotz, and then, *one* amazing present. Last year I got a new record, not scratched at all (*Highway to Hell*). Frankie got new things like clothes and a crapload of toys, developmentally appropriate for a girl three years her junior. This year I was hoping for a Walkman, although I knew it was a long shot.

Tomorrow couldn't come soon enough because we had to line up at the top of the stairs, youngest to oldest, and race down the stairs at Mom's signal. It was the best moment of our entire year. If we were willing to act like dorks, we were the happiest kids on the block. One of us kids usually woke up at the crack of dawn and got Mom and Dad out of bed. "Not yet!" Mom and Dad got up first and cooked breakfast, tormenting us with the smell of bacon and coffee. They sat and waited and made us wait until we were all in a row; then we came thundering down the stairs. I was fifteen years old, but I still did it—it was that fun—even though we knew that later in the day, things were going to get crazy.

Tory, Frankie, and I got matching Walkmans, and for the first time in history, no Barbie doll for Frankie, but she did get a giant Barbie doll–looking head to practice her hairstyling talents. Later in the week, after she had combed its synthetic hair into an electrified auburn porcupine, she declared that it had head lice and cut off all its hair while singing "Three Blind Mice." I advised her not to show Mom. It would upset her, I believed. Frankie laughed, her dark hair covering her eyes. I advised her *not* to try cutting her own hair, please just don't.

Fiona and Darcy got clothes, and Darcy started crying because almost the only thing she got was a pair of beetle black shoes. She was the only non-partier in the family, and we all stopped opening our presents and stared. Was this some kind of weird punishment?

Then Mom said, "Those are the expensive kind. You can wear them to work." Darcy stopped crying. Darcy was the practical type. She was in Army ROTC and organized her wardrobe like she was about to be deployed. She weighed the shoes in her hands, peering at the insoles. They were perfect for her job waiting on the pasty rich golfers at the Detroit Golf Club. I could see she was starting to calculate her tip money savings for college, so I turned my attention to Teresa. She was opening her presents on the sly because the quantity of liquor and cigs might be controversial. I saw that Fiona had also given her something.

"It's oregano, Mom."

When Teresa opened the giant cardboard baby doll, she started to laugh and showed everybody. Teresa named it Jesus, after her Puerto Rican boyfriend. She had finally dumped White boy Douglas, who was in prison in North Carolina for coke dealing. She could still get cute boyfriends who hadn't been to prison or who weren't the kind you edged away from when you saw them on the street hanging out. I didn't know then that she'd never have a baby, that for the rest of her life she'd be dealing with her own nightmare version of a mother's love.

She pursed her lips for a long moment, then spoke.

"That's the only baby I'll ever have," she said.

"Well, at least you don't have to change his diapers." We regarded the still-smiling baby.

"My baby." She started to cry.

"Oh, Teresa." I knew she was remembering something bad. Our bodies were young and strong and full of promise. But we didn't know we were allowed to say no, to push back. I did the only thing I knew to do.

"Have another drink, Teresa. Fuck 'em." I passed the bottle to her.

"Yeah, fuck 'em," she said and raised the bottle like a fist. "Fuck 'em all."

Love Smells like Alcohol and Looks like Jesus

Elisa, 1973

Love always smells like alcohol, looks like Jesus. When I was small, our home in Detroit would fill with people, and cases of Stroh's and Towne Club were always in plentiful supply. On the day of my first formal Holy Communion, I received a leather-bound prayer book, a puffy white dress, and rosary beads, which I wrapped around my hand as I wandered through the rooms of our home made strange by adults. Packs of children wove through the crowd with fistfuls of peanuts and potato chips, lips stained by Towne Club soda pop. The nights always ended with drinking and singing, and sometimes a fire out back, but always the singing, and always the drinking.

Jesus was crowns and stained glass and black skies with bonfires and voices in song and beer cans and Detroit and Canada and Lake Huron. Then Mom announced that Dad had always been an atheist and she was reincarnated, and Saint Michael and the crystals would make a net of light to take out the dark places in my soul, and then, just like that, Jesus was evicted, but no, the drinking and later the drugs, they stayed. And our cousins

Timothy and Floyd and Carl and Wayne died. And Teresa's friend Jacob. And Teresa went away and didn't come back for twenty-five years.

One of Those Girls

Mom, Dad, and Teresa, 1973

Before Dad's hair turned pure white, somewhere around his thirty-fifth birthday, it was the light-absorbing dark color of the Black Irish. The origin of Teresa's blond hair was an ongoing mystery.

Teresa had asked questions about a person she had started to call her "real dad" frequently enough to make Mom crazy. She looked nothing like her five matching freckled sisters, with their wavy dark auburn hair and broad peasant shoulders. She was a willow sapling set down in a grove of slow-growing oaks.

But Mom insisted that Dad was her biological father, and no sober adult ever admitted to the existence of Tommy Cassidy or the details of his murder. Teresa knew somebody was lying, but Mom's answers were consistent, whether sober or stoned on pills.

When she wondered, Teresa imagined her real father would look something like Buddy and his friends: longish hair, leather jackets, and smoking cigarettes.

Buddy was waiting for her in his car, watching Teresa with that familiar hungry gaze as she walked out of Immaculate Conception High. She climbed into the car and adjusted the hem of her too-short skirt, pretending not to notice his eyes drifting down.

"Where are we going?" she asked, reaching her hand out for the joint and taking a hit before taking a moment to register their direction. "Why aren't we going over to Belden Park?"

"Don't be a drag," he said. Teresa saw a Woodward Avenue bus shooting in the other direction, like a giant green caterpillar.

Buddy pointed the car away from the neighborhood, driving past Palmer Park's stately apartments, then into a zone where the road narrowed and neon signs and boarded-up store windows crowded the car, ready to pounce. They turned off Woodward Avenue onto a residential street with small, neat houses, but Buddy steered his car up to a small house with a torn awning and a dog tied to the front porch.

"Um. I can't stay that long today; I have to help Mom with dinner." Belden Park was enough for her; this driving outside of the neighborhood and going toward downtown was disobeying Mom and Dad at a whole new level.

"Ssh, come on." Buddy rolled his eyes. "Just be nice to my friends."

Buddy tightened his grip on her hand as they approached the back door. "Come on, Teresa."

The basement air was dank and moist, and two men on a ratty checkered couch passed a pipe back and forth. The one with the fedora and the blond goatee seemed to prickle up when she walked in. Buddy didn't introduce them. Usually Teresa liked it when boys, even men, noticed her, but she didn't like this. The hairs on the back of her neck stood up.

"Here, take a hit." Buddy let go of her hand and passed her a pipe.

"What?" She pulled her hand back, not knowing where to hold it.

"Just close your finger over the hole." He showed her how to suck in.

Teresa thought of home and her family and had a sudden longing to help Fiona with the kids, maybe ask Mom if she was OK, bringing her a glass of water and one of her little pills.

"Um," Teresa hesitated.

Buddy glanced at the men, then back at Teresa. "It's just weed," he said, so she sucked in the pipe while Buddy watched her. Teresa wondered if she was supposed to start feeling something. She didn't want to question Buddy or make him angry; he was acting weird. So she accepted her fate, pulling on the pipe and taking a sip of beer from Buddy's 40-ouncer. Her legs started to tingle and feel heavy.

"I need to sit down." She headed over to the couch.

"No, not there. Here, you should lay down." Buddy pulled her over to a corner where a mattress lay with a bristly brown pillow and a nubby green bedspread.

"Just lie down." The room was spinning, then Buddy was next to her.

"I want to go home. Buddy!" She tried to form the words. Did she say it? She must have just thought it because he didn't respond to her words at first.

"OK then," he said. She struggled against the blackness that was crowding around her temples.

"Wait..." But it was a silent plea. She had already sunk into the darkness.

She awoke to Buddy's mouth covering hers, a hand sliding under her school uniform skirt, and fingers reaching for her, probing, nails scraping her flesh. Her cheeks felt raw from being rubbed with the tiny pinpricks of Buddy's stubble, and she was barely able to breathe.

"No!" she thought. She couldn't say it, an insistent tongue. Stars and curlicues danced in the air above her, paisley circles chanting as she struggled to stay awake.

"You're my girlfriend." She tried to push him away. A prickling feeling told her that the other men in the far corner of the basement were watching them. She felt Buddy shift closer to her on the mattress. "You're not going to be a tease now, are you?" His breath smelled like smoke and old lunchmeat. She heard the zip of his pants.

The darkness was closing in like the end of a movie. She acted from instinct.

"Hey, baby." She put a hand on his arm and kissed him back, hiding her gag. Teresa looked at Buddy from beneath her lashes and registered his surprise. "Can I use the bathroom, baby?" She hoped she sounded cool enough, and soft. Teresa knew one thing—men liked to give permission. "Baby, I drank so much beer, let me use the bathroom first, baby."

Buddy nodded and pulled her up a short flight of stairs, then smacked her ass.

"Yeah, hurry up, girl." Buddy glanced down at the sea of voices. "Don't take long." She heard the flick of a lighter as he moved away as well as what he said down the stairs. "You guys hold on a minute, she's mine."

Teresa turned the water on, loud, and softly locked the flimsy eye and hook.

"Hail Mary Mother of God pray for us sinners," she murmured. If she went out the bathroom door and back down to the basement, it might be the hour of her death tonight. The window, thank God, was open, and the screen popped out easily; she hoisted herself up on the sink to the windowsill. The metal window frame rasped her thighs with a harsh scrape, but she kept her legs straight, pulling and crawling out headfirst, tumbling into the damp grass outside. Darkness had fallen, and she ran straight back through the brambles into the back alley, then turned and ran like a hunted animal. Her legs were burning, but she heard traffic ahead; she nearly ran in front of a northbound Woodward bus. It stopped, and she lunged in the door and up the metal stairs.

"Young lady?" The bus driver pointed to the fare box. "Your fare?" Then the bus driver looked down at her legs, and his face stilled into a careful expression. The bus driver's radio chirped, and he picked it up while keeping his left hand on the giant steering wheel as he drove north.

"Yep, Caucasian female, minor."

Distorted words replied.

"7 Mile, yes, coming on 7 Mile." In only a few minutes, the bus stopped with its emergency lights blinking.

Teresa sat up and looked around, still dazed. In the seats behind her, there were a few people, a dark-skinned man in a blue work shirt, and a woman with a short afro carrying a bulging purse. She met Teresa's eyes, looked down at Teresa's legs, then back up.

"You get yourself in trouble?" The woman kept looking at Teresa.

Teresa gazed down at her torn skirt, wondering what she must look like to other people. "Yes, ma'am, but I got myself out."

The woman reached into her purse and pulled out some tissues. "Here, clean yourself up."

Teresa wiped the tears from her face, then tried to straighten her skirt, brushing the dirt off. The bus door opened, and she could see the flashing lights. A uniformed Detroit police officer came in.

"Young lady, are you OK? Come off the bus." Teresa looked down at her hands; they were still bleeding. Her face was scratched, and there were long scrapes on her thighs. She climbed down the stairs shakily.

"What happened?" The officer guided her into the back of the squad car. Teresa was terrified that her parents would find out and that her family's careful performance of unity at all costs would be destroyed. Get home now, she thought.

"I fell," she whispered, looking down.

"You fell, you say? You sure?"

"Um, yes. I, I fell," she repeated.

The officer glanced at her face, then down at her bleeding legs. "You shouldn't be by yourself. Things happen," he said.

The other officer's greasy white scalp reflected the dim light. "Wearing an Immaculate Conception uniform? Look what you got yourself into." He adjusted himself behind the steering wheel.

The other one spoke. "Let's bring this one home." He added, "Where do you live sweetheart?"

Teresa choked out her address, unsteady again.

The cops drove her toward home, lights out, not flashing.

"University District? Unbelievable. Can't believe these little Catholic girls going down to Highland Park on a school night." The squad car turned onto Teresa's street.

They didn't speak to her as she climbed out of the car and walked up to the door. There would be no police report. It was 11 o'clock. She was seven hours late getting home from school, but they were right on time for an end-of-shift drink.

Teresa walked in the side door. Mom was sitting on the kitchen bench.

"Mom!" She ran toward her. "Buddy attacked me!"

Mom put her hands out, warding her off. "Stop." She looked Teresa up and down. "Your father is out looking for you. Go take a bath right now. Hurry. Don't let him see any of this." Mom's voice had a cold edge to it.

Teresa reeled back in shock but obeyed.

The water burned as she sank into the tub and scrubbed, the bristly washcloth chafing her skin until the only visible trace of her night were her skinned knees and hands.

Dad and Mom were at the kitchen table.

Mom spoke quickly. "It was extremely irresponsible of you to fall sleep at your friend's house without calling us or telling her parents you were there. Didn't you care if we're worried about you?"

Dad spoke carefully. "We have a pretty good thing going here with seven of us." He said seven people. If you counted Teresa, there were eight.

Dad continued. "You out until eleven o'clock with a friend I didn't even know about. And her parents either? Her father or brother should have walked you home. I don't even know why you have a friend who doesn't even ask her parents if she can have company." Dad had a strange look on his face. "Bad things happen to girls, Teresa. To good girls and to loose girls." His hand was shaking.

"Don't be one of those girls, Teresa." And then, as if a light had suddenly switched off, he turned away.

She looked at Dad, but he didn't see her. He only saw her blond hair, and he didn't count her. He wasn't her dad. Teresa wished just two things. One, she wanted to look at another person, just once, and see her own reflection there; to know where she belonged. And just once, she wanted to hear her mom tell her the truth.

Teresa turned to her mother, hoping for comfort. Mom sat like a statue, hands splayed on the yellow Formica table. Teresa climbed the stairs before they could turn into fists. She passed her own door and slipped into her littlest sisters' bedroom, where they lay piled like puppies on the giant foam mattress. Teresa curled up at their feet, close enough to feel their warmth, to hear their soft breathing. She didn't sleep for a long time.

Family of Origin: The 1950s

Cold Case Detroit

My Darling

Girl in Blue

Meat

Penthouse Living

Cold Case Detroit

Dad, 1953

When my paternal grandfather died after a six-week bout of leukemia, my father and his four siblings were separated and sent to live and work on neighboring farms in Ontario, Canada. My grandmother moved to Detroit with my oldest aunt, and they both worked until they could reunite the family there. Dad moved to Detroit's east side to finish his middle and high school years.

```
REPORT OF MISSING PERSON
Date: January 3, 1953
Time: 10:18 P.M.
Received by: Patrolman Richard Condit
Last Name: Gillespie First Name: Joann
MI.C.
Address: 2931 Fisher Detroit MI
Occupation: Student
Last seen at: Kercheval and Fisher
Date: 1/2/53
Time: 9:30 P.M.
```

Dennis didn't date. He'd asked out Joann, his little sister's best friend once, but that had been a sweaty-palmed, stuttering failure. Dennis thought Joann was a perfect girl. He had memorized her legs, the way her plaid Saint Charles of Detroit skirt just touched her knees; her wrists, delicate and pale, visible because of her too short uniform sleeves; her dark, wavy hair.

"You're like a big brother to me," she had cooed. "You're so cute." That sentence was the most frustrating and confusing one he'd heard from a girl ever. If only little sisters and their friends were as easy to figure out as math.

Dennis studied engineering at Wayne State University; he was the college boy with the dubious task of leading the math homework sessions for his little sister and her best friend. Annie and Joann were too old to need him to walk them to the bus stop, but not too old to act the part of giggling students, dragging out study sessions. So that winter evening in Detroit, after another frustrating hour and a half of "tutoring," Joann and Annie swished away toward the Jefferson Avenue trolley stop and the 6 o'clock show at the Deluxe. They were dressed for a September evening, not this cold January night. Joann's legs were pale and curvy beneath her black woolen skirt, and Annie's coat was unbuttoned over her thin summer blouse.

"For God's sake, Dennis," said Annie. "We're eighteen." She paused. "Besides, we'll be walking together." Joann shared a glance with Annie for a moment before both girls turned and walked away into the winter twilight. Dennis wondered. Were they meeting someone? Is that why they had shrugged him off?

```
REPORT OF MISSING PERSON
PHYSICAL DESCRIPTION
Sex: Female
Color: White
Nativity: French Irish
Age: 18
Height: 5' 2"
Weight: 120
Eyes: Brown
Hair: Dark Brown
Religion: Catholic
Teeth Peculiarities: Good
Physical Condition: Good
Mental Condition: Good
```

Darkness never fully descended in Detroit in the winter. The snow on the tiny patchwork of lawns reflected the light of the streetlamps. The girls have gone to plenty of movies, Dennis reassured himself.

He climbed the stairs to their flat and stepped over to the front window. Dennis couldn't stop himself from watching them walk down Baldwin, past the dingy row of houses that, like theirs, had been divided into flats during the war. From this angle, Joann and Annie looked more like grade school girls, not young women. If only he was a little taller, like his brother Tim, with straight hair, not nearsighted and with hair so unruly his boss at the restaurant told him, "Get a haircut, you look like a girl." Even Joann's big brother Nick had gotten his growth spurt.

I might as well study. Dennis shrugged and picked up his engineering textbook. It weighed a hundred times more than his journalism textbooks had. But this was Detroit. You either built the car or designed the car. If not, you fed, cleaned up after, or taught the children of the people who did.

Dennis turned so he didn't have to look at the empty sidewalk and walked back over to the kitchen table and clicked on the light.

The lamp created a small and luminous place, there at the kitchen table. And here was his textbook, filled with puzzles he could solve. It was satisfying to set down a neat row of lines and numbers with a sharpened pencil. But when Dennis was done, nothing changed. He imagined the years ahead; row upon row of problems to solve and theories to memorize. They were a grim platoon of purposeful soldiers, insisting he keep up.

He'd rather imagine the moment when Annie would come up the stairs and run to the phone to talk to Joann Gillespie, to tell her that yes, she had made it down Baldwin to home and was Joann coming over tomorrow, because tomorrow was Saturday and they could do their homework together, and yes, Dennis would be there, because Dennis knows math, and yes, we can get him to help us, and, "Dennis, you'll be home tomorrow, won't you?" Dennis smiled.

And then happiness would be nesting right there in the kitchen, like a bright tropical bird. Joann Gillespie in a skirt, sitting at the kitchen table, her plump calf curled around a chair leg, lips candy pink, teeth straight and white, chewing on a pencil eraser and asking him to please, explain that again, and, "Dennis, you're sooo smart."

Dennis started from his reverie as his older sisters Megan and Elizabeth clattered up the stairs. It was payday, and they had stopped at Sam's Cut Rate on their way home from work at the hospital.

"Where's Annie? She has to try these on. We bought her some boots."

```
REPORT OF MISSING PERSON
DESCRIPTION OF DRESS
Overcoat: Tan
Skirt: Black
Sweater: White
Shoes: White Oxfords
Stockings: White Socks
Money carried: $10.00
Reported Missing By: Alice Gillespie
Relationship: Mother
Address: 2931 Fisher Detroit MI
Telephone: WA-400244
```

Dennis tilted his head toward the stairs as Annie, almost right behind them, brought in a draft of January cold as she shrugged out of her thin coat, shivering.

"Hi, Annie, how was the show?" Dennis raised his voice over Elizabeth and Megan's laughter.

"Come on, Annie. Try them on!" Elizabeth, usually the serious one, was giggling and holding out a pair of boots to Annie.

Dennis held his hands up and pretended to be holding a camera. He pressed his index finger down on an imaginary button.

"Smile," he said. "You look wonderful." Then Dennis lowered his hands. "Annie, doesn't Joann usually call by now?"

REPORT OF MISSING PERSON
ADDITIONAL INFORMATION
JoAnn Gillespie and Anne Sinnett, a girl
friend, went to the DeLuxe Theatre, 9355
Kercheval, at 6:00 on the evening of
January 2nd. They left the Theatre at 9:00
P.M. and walked to Kercheval and Fischer,
where they separated. They had an
understanding that JoAnn was to call Anne
when she reached home which was their
custom when they went out together to
ensure that everything was all right. Anne
called JoAnn and found out that she had
not reached home yet, whereupon the
parents called the Police Department and a
missing report was issued at 11:00 P.M. In
spite of the apparent seriousness of the
call, according to the write up, the scout
car responding to the missing person call
did nothing to further enlist the aid of
other officers, nor was the information
reported to the D.B. Inspector at that
time.

"Maybe she forgot. Or was it my turn to call?" Annie's fingers were already dialing the phone. Nick picked up.

"I don't know. About ten minutes. I'm not positive, Nick." Dennis was listening to Annie's replies. Annie held the phone out, her head turned to one side. She was still holding the receiver when a few minutes later there was a loud knock and Joann's brother Nick was at the door.

"Dennis, Joann didn't make it home."

"Let me grab my coat," Dennis answered. Then, "Annie, hang up the phone. Sit down. We're going to go find Joann." Annie turned to him, a confused look on her face. Megan gently took the phone from Annie and placed it back in its cradle.

"Sit down, Annie. They'll be right back."

Dennis followed Nick down the stairs, and they stood on the sidewalk, their breath coming out in puffs. The night was bitter cold now.

"Where would she have gone?" Dennis asked. Saying it, he knew the answer.

"Nowhere," Nick said.

They started walking, shoulder to shoulder, briskly, toward the corner where the girls usually parted.

They worked their way up and down the empty sidewalk, looking between each house, calling. Dennis could see the streetlamp in front of the Gillespies' flat down the long tunnel of trees.

"Let's go back and look in the alley," Nick said. "Joann!"

"Joann!" Dennis echoed.

Dennis had never thought that the alley was unfriendly before. Boys were always allowed to walk through it, even after dark. The people in their windows would be silhouetted against the night, having ordinary lives. There would be houses with fathers still alive, families sitting around a table with a feed of some Friday night fish and chips, and apartments with lights dimmed and a couple pressed together, dancing. But tonight, the windows were unblinking eyes. Only Nick and Dennis were out here, alone and calling for Joann Gillespie.

Dennis was walking along the left side of the alley, peering into the backyards.

"Nick?" He stopped.

They were behind the rooming house, a four-story building. Its back door and yard were in shadows.

"There's something over there." There. Beside the tool shed.

Dennis saw her legs first.

He felt Nick's hand gripping his forearm.

Her skirt was pushed all the way up, and something dark stained the snowy ground beneath her. Her face, her lovely face, was cold, and her coat was open. Joann Gillespie was lying in the snow. There in the snow.

"Nick, stay back."

Dennis stepped forward, then knelt in the snow beside her, laying his shaking fingers on her neck, searching for her pulse. There was something wrong with her neck.

Dennis bowed his head, the words of the Hail Mary forming on his lips. *Mother of God, pray for us.*

"Nick, go get your dad."

SUBJECT: Fatal Assault and Rape of JoAnn Gillespie, 2931 Fischer, January 3, 1953

The above girl went to the Deluxe Theater with a girlfriend who lives at 1820 Baldwin. Phone number L0-7-8896. They parted at Kercheval and Fisher and were to call each other when they got home. The above girl was found murdered in Alley next to the garage at 2543 Fisher by Dennis Sinnett.

The brothers, father and other persons who were friends of the missing girl conducted a search of the neighborhood and found the body of JoAnn near the alley at the rear of 2543 Fischer. The police were called and at 10:46 P.M. scout 5-3 responded. At 10:25 the Belle Isle Radio Operator called the D.B. Desk and stated that Homicide Officers were wanted at the scene where the dead girl was found in the alley and that she had been beaten. The D.B. Inspector did not get in touch with the patrolmen who responded in scout car 5-3 and had the officer and the D.B. Inspector conversed together over the telephone, details of the crime could have been secured much quicker than resulted from the procedure employed.

The first teletype was sent out at 2:38
A.M. on teletype 47 for all officers to be
on the alert for anyone having blood on
clothing or scratched as possible suspects
in the murder of the subject. A question
is raised as to why a radio broadcast and
teletype was not put out immediately
concerning the death of the girl for the
information of all scout cars and
officers.

My Darling

Mom, Tommy, and Jolene, 1954

Marie's seen this car before, in the front parking lot of the Willis Baptist where every month she and her family have to get dressed up and wait in line for small miracles in the form of pasta, canned spinach, and day-old bread. Mom doesn't even notice, but boys, even men, look at her. They drive past and make low whistling sounds at girls waiting with their mothers for commodity food and the discards of the Believers. It wasn't so bad when they were in elementary school. But Marie is older now, and she needs new clothes. Her skirts have been steadily creeping up her legs until now they are almost midthigh, and the boys notice, they say things.

"Hey, church girl!" It's Thursday, after school. Marie keeps up her pace and looks straight ahead to where the buses are parked. A quick glance tells her that it's one of those cars, the 1956 powder blue Ford Fairlane convertible to be exact. She hears a car door slam, footsteps slapping across the pavement.

"Hey." Tommy Cassidy is standing right in front of her. He feints as if to put his finger under her chin and force it up, but then pauses and instead smooths down his reddish-blond hair. "I'm just kidding."

"Oh, okay." She glances down at his hand and then fixes him with a long, hard glare.

"How else can a fellow get a pretty girl to talk to him? Don't be stingy," he said.

Stingy? She wasn't stingy. This statement made her pause long enough to allow him to steer her into the front seat of his ride, as if they knew each other well, and this was a predetermined meeting.

"Do you know how to drive?" he asked her, sliding the Fairlane out of Park and pulling out onto Packard Avenue. "You're so grown up and pretty for a high school girl," Tommy said as he put his arm around her in one smooth movement. She didn't protest.

This was not a high school boy. This was Tommy Cassidy. He had been at the consolidated school when Marie was a pudgy seventh-grader with a haircut by Mom involving a bowl and dull scissors. It was easier to get the head lice out when you could get behind the ears and neck. Tommy had been in the upper school, but he didn't walk at graduation. Marie knew because he had been one of the wild boys hanging around with her oldest brother, and people said there was something about the principal's niece and the auditorium after play practice had ended. Tommy had been expelled from school for the infraction they said he committed at the school—not like her brother who only committed infractions at home, and he never had to pay for those.

But things were better now that she was in tenth grade. She knew how to take care of herself. Marie had a lock on her door and a mirror; she cut her own hair, styled into a pixie cut. She had one chipped tooth, but her teeth were clean; she brushed them religiously with salt and baking soda and her finger. She was not going to have a stinking mouth like Mother. She had a shoebox full of different clip-on earrings, bracelets, even a pair of nylons and a red lipstick.

Now this boy, really this man, had called her pretty. Maybe this time it would be different, maybe she could make things go her way.

"What's your name, darling?" he asked, drawing her in closer.

"You know who I am." She looked at him sideways, trying to gauge his reaction.

"I do, actually," he said. "You're Cody's cute little sister," he added. "But you're all grown up. Can I take you for a little drive before I take you home?" He already was turning the wrong direction at the corner. "We'll get a pop."

Marie didn't think anything she could say would make a difference, so she started imagining the taste of a Faygo on her tongue. It had been so long since she had tasted a pop, and yet here was Tommy driving up and down Michigan Avenue down the cruise route that the boys liked to take with their cars to show off. They pulled up to a red light and saw another car with a boy and girl together in the front seat. Tommy pulled Marie in closer, then looked to the other car to see if anyone had noticed. It was one of the football players from school and a girl Marie didn't know dressed in a cotton blouse with a strand of pearls. Of course she had on no makeup, not like Marie, who always liked to apply lipstick and face powder the second she stepped on the school bus. Tommy nodded at the other boy, and the boy had to nod back because Tommy used to play football at Lincoln, and the Ford Fairlane was the far and away superior car. Marie wondered idly how he could afford it. Marie avoided making eye contact with the proper female companion sitting on the far side of the car, hands folded in her lap. There wasn't a chance she would even speak to Marie should they meet at school, in the bathroom at a football game, anywhere. Marie knew the routine, she knew that it was her cue to laugh, look up at Tommy, and act the part of an adoring girlfriend. That's how it worked. You had to make them happy, make them look good in front of other boys. And if you did that, well, then maybe he would actually be your boyfriend.

Tommy steered the big car down Stadium Street and past the University of Michigan football stadium, and then back toward Ypsilanti. He didn't talk, and Marie sensed a change in his mood, so she pretended to be interested in the radio. "Do you mind?" she asked and punched the buttons until she found a familiar song. They listened in silence to the Everly Brothers, and after a while Tommy seemed to be less tense and they pulled into Bea's. He seemed to have an instinct about these things. The drive-in was now filled with cars, he had the best car, he had Marie tucked under his arm, and he drove the length of the parking lot of the drive-in restaurant before he parked and leaned toward the speaker.

"You want some fries, babe? A burger? A drink?"

Marie shouldn't be surprised he was already calling her "babe."

"Oh, sure, whatever you're having," She knew she was supposed to pretend that she wasn't hungry. "It sounds great." She spoke in an even tone, but she was salivating. She hoped he wanted more than a Faygo pop. It was near the end of the month, and the food box had all but run out; they had been eating the same potato soup with hamburger grease for the last four days.

"Okay then, two burgers, two fries, two Faygos," Tommy ordered. Marie felt almost faint at the thought of food but waited as if she didn't have a care in the world, leaning toward Tommy with interest as he talked.

"Yes, they're going to dig some gravel pits, right behind your house, I heard Lloyd Beloit say so, you can't stop progress they say." Marie nodded, but her eyes were on the carhop coming toward them. She hoped Jolene might be working tonight. They hadn't seen each other after school. It was Jolene, dark haired and curvy with her signature bright red lipstick.

She brought the tray over, set it down, and smiled. "Here's your food, hon." She looked over, then saw Marie. "Marie!" Jolene looked surprised.

"I didn't realize you were working today," Marie responded.

Tommy looked from girl to girl; for a moment his gaze hung suspended, then Jolene turned quickly toward Tommy and said, "Will you be needing anything else, doll?" She'd turned her attention back to him and pulled two straws from her apron and some paper napkins. "Extra ketchup?"

Tommy relaxed, and Marie clasped her hands together and pursed her lips. Tommy pulled out a wad of bills and threw a few at Jolene. "Keep the change," he said.

"Thanks, handsome," she said to Tommy.

Before she sashayed away, Jolene curled her three middle fingers down and splayed her pinky and thumb out, making a telephone out of her hand, held it up to her head, and mouthed "call me" to Marie. Marie made the a-okay signal. Tommy looked up from folding his money back into his wallet, but Marie was already opening a paper napkin on her lap.

"I didn't know you knew Jolene," he said.

"Oh, yes, she's a great girl," Marie said, "really great."

Marie kept her voice light, then held out her hands for the cardboard tray.

When Tommy passed the food over, Marie forced herself to eat slowly, chewing each rich and salty bite. She sucked the salt off the fries before she chewed them, then pulled on the pop, cold, cool heaven.

Tommy was watching her. "You enjoying those?" he asked.

Marie was embarrassed. "Oh, yes, thank you, I just..." She didn't know what to say. If he could just leave the car and leave her with the burger and fries and maybe a chance to talk to Jolene, it would be fine with her. But she should stop thinking silly thoughts. You were supposed to focus on the boy, they liked that.

"It's so cool of you to bring me here today." But if Marie knew boys, there would be a price for this meal, sooner or later. Right now she didn't care. Maybe she should wrap up half of the burger and give it to her little sister Rita. But no, Mom would never let Rita go hungry. Whatever there was to save, some potato flakes, a last bit of butter, or an egg, it would be saved for Rita.

"It's nice to see a girl who doesn't just pick at her food," Tommy said. He picked up a fry from his plate, moved it around in her ketchup, and popped it in his mouth. "You don't mind sharing, do you?"

She wasn't sure what to answer, but he seemed content to keep talking. "I have something to share with you," he continued. "Do you want something to liven up your Faygo?" Tommy was pouring a strong-smelling liquid into his cup. Marie didn't, but it was important to be game. Boys let you know what they wanted, and it usually was easier if they were happy. She mourned a little the sparkling clean black cherry taste, but she said yes. She spluttered when she tasted it, and Tommy laughed; she saw that he liked that she did not know how to drink.

It was strong, but then she felt warmth in her throat, spreading to her toes. Tommy pulled her to him and kissed her.

"Cool it a little, okay?" Marie said. She saw Jolene come back to pick up the trays and took the opportunity to scoot back a little. Marie and Jolene shared a glance, and Jolene rolled her eyes. Marie giggled. Jolene took their tray and went back to the little stand.

"Now what are you doing way over there, baby?" Tommy kept asking questions. "What do you say we go out Friday night? I can take you over to the show, maybe even out for Italian, dress up."

Marie thought about it. She drank the last of the soda and nodded. "But Mom won't let me go out with you." She knew her mom would say no if she asked. She was only fifteen, and she knew since Tommy was her brother's friend, he was already twenty or twenty-one.

"Pick me up at Jolene's house instead." Mr. and Mrs. Rollo were always glued to the TV, and they never seemed to notice if Marie was there; it was a relaxing change. "Mr. and Mrs. Rollo won't mind."

*

On Friday night when it was time to go to Jolene's house, Marie was ready. She turned around in her small bedroom. The floor was cracked linoleum, and the top of her head barely cleared the wood strips nailed in to keep the thick sheets of plastic in place over the high, small windows. The plastic was an addition after the former tenants, the chickens, vacated the premises. Marie saw the path leading to the gravel pit site and the railroad tracks like a wavering, blurry line going nowhere. The whole town of Willis, Michigan, was like that. The Pickle Barrel Inn and

Tavern and the railroad tracks made up most of the town, and one dirt road led toward Ypsilanti, where the children took the school bus into the town; the other dirt road led in the direction of the freeway side road and the Willow Run defense plant. A few families had managed to get into the plant, beating out the southerners coming up to work on the bombers. Some were able to keep their farms, or at least the farmhouses, and one family still had horses.

But Marie's family didn't have a worker in the plant, and their house was the former outbuilding of the house next door. Set back from the road, it was actually two chicken coops clapped together and held in place with tar paper. It was stifling in the summer and freezing in the winter. This was where Marie, her mother, Ruth, and her brothers and sisters moved when Marie was seven. She missed the brick house near the Huron River and the paper factory. Mom smiled a lot more when they lived in town, and her brothers weren't afraid to ask her for things at the grocery store when they all went to the neighborhood Wrigley's.

But after Daddy left, the boys at first became surly and whiney, always asking for meat, complaining their legs hurt, their heads hurt, their teeth hurt—anything to get the girls' share of the meat—but then they got nasty. They never stopped bothering her, pinching her, punching her, and Cody. Cody liked to rub up against her when she was in her nightie, the same as Daddy. Nasty like Daddy until Mama had made Daddy leave, smashing him in the face with his own saxophone, ripping his cheek with a deep gash.

And now Marie made sure she always had a boyfriend and a lock on her door. This Tommy was no boy, but it was time for her to get another boyfriend. Cody was getting that look in his eye again, and she had heard him standing outside her door. She began to pull her little sister Rita into the bed with her; she didn't want Cody to get any new ideas. She didn't really like doing things with boys; she thought they were disgusting with their insistant pushing and preening and sensitivities. She could hold off for a long time—it was easy to make the high school boys wait a long time—but she knew she was getting a reputation. The girls at school made sure of that, and she didn't think Tommy was the type to wait for something he wanted. But having Tommy as a boyfriend would have its good side.

That's what she told Jolene later when she was putting the finishing touches on her makeup in Jolene's bedroom as Jolene combed out her curls.

"Well, do you really need another boyfriend so soon?" The girls were looking at each other in the mirror.

"Jolene, you know, I can't stop thinking about Jeanine." Jolene nodded, tearing up. Jeannine had been different, different like them; she just hadn't been as good at hiding it as Jolene and Marie. Jeanine had been attacked after school; her parents had pulled her from the school and moved to Ohio.

Jolene's eyes were gray and flat. "I know, Marie, I know." She stroked Marie's hair with a brush, slow strokes. "It's just, he's not like the high school boys, you're going to have to..." Her eyes filled with tears.

Marie spoke. "And at least he doesn't go to our school. We won't have anyone to bug us all day."

Jolene sighed, then giggled. "Your last boyfriend was too much!" They both laughed, remembering the boy who had a crush on Marie. They called him Blinky because he stared at her so much. Blinky had followed the girls around everywhere and waited for Marie after every class and insisted on escorting her down the high school halls like she was a member of the royal family. Jolene and Marie didn't get a moment together, not even to share one piece of gossip, that Blinky wouldn't want in on. And sometimes if you just told boys to bug off, it made things worse.

Blinky was a perfect boyfriend in some respects, but when his family found out who he was dating, they were finished. No one like Marie for the fine families of Ypsilanti, Michigan.

Jolene sniffled.

"I just can't stand the thought of him touching you like that." Jolene walked over to her bedroom door and sat down, barricading anyone from entering. Marie walked over to her and held Jolene as she cried. Jolene sniffled. "I wish, I wish." Marie patted her head to comfort her.

"I know, I know," she said softly into Jolene's hair, "but I'm here now." Then Marie's lips were soft on Jolene's, and the girls kissed, straining their bodies toward each other. Marie pulled away first, although she continued to hug Jolene.

"We'll never get out of here," said Jolene, defeated.

"We will, Jolene. We'll get out," Marie said. The girls heard a commotion at the door, and they knew Tommy was probably sitting in the living room with Jolene's daddy.

The girls stood up quickly, and Jolene checked Marie's curls. Jolene laid her hand on Marie's cheek for a brief moment, tucked a stray wisp of hair behind her ear. Marie felt rather than heard Jolene's goodbye.

"Have a good night, darling," she whispered.

Girl in Blue

Dad, Mom, and Tommy, 1958

Dennis was seven years past his high school sweetheart's murder when he first saw Marie in the lobby of the defense lab. His technical skills had conscripted him into helping with the Korea "situation." Marie had a "situation" too, which gifted her with the psychic prescience that Dennis was the man she had to marry.

Dennis hadn't thought that far ahead. He was nervous around women, even though he had a professional job and had almost finished college. Marie Benoit was in the secretarial pool, and he had the right to walk straight up to her and hand her a sheaf of papers and numbers to type up.

"Hello, Miss Benoit," he always stuttered.

"Helloooooo Mr. Sinnett." She would draw out his name, mocking his inflection a little bit. "Don't you get a little bored of all these figures? What do you talk to girls about when you take them out? Or do you just follow them around the lunchroom?" She smiled at him.

She exercised the only power she had ever known in her life—red lipstick—and the office dress code just barely followed. One more button undone, skirt hiked up just a little when she crossed her legs. Those nylons were difficult to keep free of runs; she lived in fear of that and having to go bare-legged until payday.

Dennis thought about the last time a girl had flirted with him; it had been a long time. He lingered at Marie's desk a bit longer than necessary, then hastened away. Neil, the engineer he reported to, glanced his way with a grimace.

"You better watch yourself with that one," Neil warned. "Those girls from Willow Run, in the shacks by the plant. They might have nice tits, but be careful, that's all I'm saying. Don't even think about getting involved."

Dennis didn't tell Neil that he'd already organized his lunchtime around the typist two times in a row and sat at Marie's table, even managed a "hello." Neil droned on, but Dennis was lost in thought. Her scent was like wildflowers, her legs thick and curvy.

"Oh, forget it," Neil said. "Go check the code again."

Dennis didn't think of Marie again until he saw her standing outside the gate at quitting time. She wore white gloves and a light blue dress. She looked like Easter. Suddenly he felt brave.

"Aren't you a little young to be working here?" he blurted.

"Now why would you be wanting to know how old I am?"

"Umm..." he started.

"Don't you worry, I'm legal. I just don't have a ride home." She was perfectly still, holding her breath.

"Where are you going?" Dennis took her elbow, surprising himself.

She waited until they were driving to answer him.

"We can go wherever you want." She said it in the carefree voice she had been affecting as she lit her cigarette, but her hands were shaking. There was a lot at stake.

Dennis felt the night opening up with a sense of unexpected mystery. Anything could happen, good things. Marie felt her rib cage expand as she took a deep, relieved breath.

"It's too soon to go home," he said. "There's more to life than work and sleep." Dennis had never uttered a sentence like this in his life, but with Marie smiling up at him, it felt natural. He hadn't stammered once.

He turned right on Michigan Avenue, toward the city, away from Marie's home.

"Hey, that's a nice car." Dennis nodded at the powder blue convertible pulling alongside them. The driver didn't return his nod. "That someone you know?" Dennis asked. "He seems to know you."

"Oh, no, that's just some stupid friend of my brother's. Don't worry about it."

The car kept pace with them for a few blocks. Marie stared straight ahead. She kept breathing. As they passed the giant Eastern Michigan University water tower, the blue car receded. Marie checked her lipstick in her compact, searching for a flash of blue. Tommy's message was clear. He didn't want her, but he wasn't done with her either. She rubbed her sweater across her middle. She wasn't sure which way her gamble was going to go.

Marie turned toward Dennis. She knew the routine, knew to laugh, look up at Dennis, and act adoring. That's how it worked. You had to keep them excited. She set her hand on Dennis's leg and moved it up his thigh slightly.

"Maybe there's a show at the Albion?" A drive-in—that could solve all her problems.

Dennis smiled. He wasn't the kind of guy that girls really looked at twice, let alone the kind of guy a girl went out with twice. Trying to make conversation with ordinary girls exhausted him. They were too neat, too well-mannered, and so proper. Their idea of a big disaster was not being able to find a good song on the radio or having too much ice in their cola. He could scarcely get to the end of a date—let alone a second or a third. The truth was, his heart still belonged to Joann Gillespie.

For months after the murder, Joann's older brother and Dennis stood guard on the porch every night with their shotguns, responding to death threats made against Dennis's little sister, who'd been with Joann that night. In spite of the protection they tried to provide, standing vigil on the porch, these death threats had gotten through to Annie. "We're going to get you next."

When Annie tried to lead a normal life, going back to school, she'd been followed. The threat was real, and after more than one hundred arrests and thirteen false confessions, the detectives gave it up as a cold case. The monster that had raped and killed the first girl that Dennis had ever loved walked free, but Dennis never would, and neither would Annie. He'd found Joann too late, had touched her neck to find a pulse, but her skin was cold, and he couldn't save her. That night Dennis had cried noiselessly and retched as he placed a sweater under her head. He'd covered her with his coat. He loved her still.

Whenever he met a new girl, Joann's face flashed before his, five minutes after he had met them, fifteen minutes, five hours. It didn't matter. Sooner or later she would say or do something that reminded him in some small way of Joann. It startled girls, the way he would suddenly stop speaking in the middle of a sentence, his eyes drifting to the left. One of his ill-fated dates had said to him, "You look as if you're at a funeral." Another had said, "You're just too depressing, Dennis." He hadn't tried with a girl for a long while. It was impossible.

But right here was a girl, short and dark haired, sitting next to him on this seat, looking at her compact, painting on a giant red kiss, letting him know she was game to go to the drive-in. "It might get chilly later," he answered. "But maybe I can keep you warm." Dennis put his arm around her and pulled her into his chest. Just let people see him now, turning into the drive-in with a pretty girl hanging on to him, her hand on his leg. Only Marie saw the blue car pull in behind them.

Marie sensed Tommy's presence, like the electricity sparking in the air when a predator was nearby. She learned this feeling early with her father, then her brothers. The hair prickled on the nape of her neck. She knew Tommy was waiting to talk to her.

"Think, Marie, think." She looked over at Dennis, still wearing his tie from work, his cheek peppered with small nicks and cuts as if he had trouble shaving that morning. He smelled like fresh soap and was doing that bragging thing boys did, talking about how important his job was to national security. She hoped there wouldn't be a quiz later.

"So the postcard came from Russia. That's behind the Iron Curtain." This was the strangest thing a man had ever said to her. She wasn't sure what he was talking about, but a vague memory from senior history class stirred. She leaned forward and stretched her face into a smile, nodding. She hoped he could see how enamored she was of him, because this baby growing inside of her needed a father, and Marie had a deadline.

Dennis leaned back against the car window as if he had just run around the block and needed to cool down. She saw the pulse beating at his neck. Dennis was nervous, but not for the same reason as Marie. She knew only one sure way to get a guy's attention, and it must be the same for the smart ones too. She moved in and accidentally brushed his inner pant leg, felt his response under her hand, then moved it to his chest. She knew she'd gotten his attention, and he wouldn't be going anywhere for a while.

"Dennis, I'm just going to the ladies room. I'll be right back." Her hand brushed him again, then she climbed out of the car. Marie knew he'd be waiting for her when she got back, no matter how long it took her. She went to find Tommy.

As Marie walked between the rows of cars in the gravel parking lot, she pulled her gloves off. Her hands were slippery. She adjusted the earrings that were starting to dig into the soft flesh of her earlobes, ran her hands through her hair. She breathed in the scent of lilacs and the smell of summer heat rising. Spring ended so abruptly, without warning. One day all the lilacs and forsythias were blooming as if they were children wearing bright clothes, running on a school yard, then the next they were desiccated and brown, rotting on the branch.

Maybe her maneuver tonight could conjure a future into existence. Tommy's car was at the very edge of the parking lot, the dimness of twilight increased by the presence of the weeping willow, overgrown with drooping vines. It was parked so far back that the trunk was flush against the tree branches that hung like a stage curtain over the back of the car. She heard rustling behind the leaves and hesitated, then saw Tommy appear, sipping a strong-smelling drink from a paper cup.

"Why'd you follow me, Tommy? What do you want?" She felt terrified to speak to him like this, but it was her last chance. "Are you jealous?" She could only hope.

"So what are you doing with the little professor boy?" He didn't answer her question.

"Tommy." She placed one hand on her belly and one hand on his arm, fine red hair almost invisible, freckled yet tan. She gulped.

"You know I'm expecting." There was nothing to lose.

"Yeah, well, babe, I told you, it's too soon to get tied down. I have a lot to do. Here, hold on." He wrote something down on a piece of paper, handed it to her, took another sip from his cup. Marie's stomach turned at the harsh-smelling liquid.

She squinted down at the penciled-in phone number.

"What?"

"Here, Marie." He pressed something into her hand, and she looked down at the crisp stack of twenty-dollar bills. "Call this number, this doctor will take care of that little problem for you."

She gazed at the total value of her life and her child's life combined.

"Problem?" Her tactic—no, her hope—had failed her.

"It's better this way, Marie. We used to have so much fun; and you're so pushy now." He pulled her to him in a one-armed hug, then turned away. His eyes were already scanning the parking lot. "Go back to your professor, Miss Marie."

Marie stumbled back as he brushed past her. In a trance, she pulled her dirty glove out of her small white pocketbook. She wiped the dust from her shoes, freshened up her lipstick, and adjusted her sky blue coat. Taking a deep breath, she invoked a sashay into her step, mentally rehearsing lines for her next big scene.

Meat

Marie, 1955

The back yard shimmered with the late July heat. The boy sat on the submarine-shaped propane gas tank lazily aiming his BB gun at the back window of the garage. He aimed, pretended to shoot, then wheeled around and pointed it at his sister, fat Marie. She carried a white enameled pot half-filled with water, trying to pour it on her bedraggled collection of gardenias. The water slopped everywhere, mud trickled and pooled in front of the graying and splintered back steps.

"Watch what you're doing, fatty!" he shouted at her.

Marie always got the last slurp of the greasy soup gravy when she washed the pots. No wonder she was so fat. It would be easy to shoot her, but he didn't. He knew he wasn't supposed to shoot at people, but Dad wasn't around anymore. He swiveled the rifle around and pointed it toward the patch of woods behind the house leading to the gravel pit. Maybe he could get a rabbit. They hadn't had meat in a long time, not since before school let out at least. He set his rifle down on his bony knees with a sigh. His stomach rumbled.

Marie bent down and pulled a weed from the flowerbed, humming under her breath. She didn't speak to her brother, but she glanced at the rifle now and then. "Mom would kill him," she thought. She grabbed the pot and walked to the edge of the woods. Maybe she could find some wild apples or chickweed for dinner. She thought of Jolene's record, *Top Hits! From 1955*. She sang aloud the farther she got away from the house, "Mr. Sandman, bring me a dream."

Penthouse Living

Marie, 2006

I had a dream last night that I was living in the Jeffries projects, the big orange buildings you can see from John C. Lodge Freeway in Detroit, where Motown artist Diana Ross grew up. I was alone in bed, looking at a black-and-white photo, waiting for someone named Felix to call me, but the phone never rang. I woke up wondering if my dream was about a past lifetime—it was far too close to the life I'm living now.

I fell asleep looking at my family photo album again. That happens easily now; the Vicodin tires me out, and I don't have a couch because the apartment is too small. For relaxing, it's the yellow armchair from Renee's place or the bed. Renee never calls, and it feels like I'm always waiting for her, but she lives with Janet now. Ailene never calls either. She won't even go to a party or to a workshop if she knows I'll be there. I apologized to her. I sent her presents. I sent her an email. I called her, but she never called back. She wouldn't let me explain that the tumor in my brain made me act that way, and now it's gone. But it made no difference. A week after the news made it out to the EarthDream network that my MRI was clear, she stopped calling me. Her feelings of obligation were through, and so were we.

Now I'm perched above the world in my fifteenth-story penthouse apartment in the Pleasant Oak senior high rise. I can see from Canada to Pontiac. The rent is only $160—subsidized housing, they call it—and it's clean and safe. But I'm still alone and waiting for someone to call. Today I'm waiting for Elisa, who promised to take me shopping at Trader Joe's. I missed the senior shuttle yesterday because I thought today was Tuesday. But it's Wednesday, and today the shuttle is going to Meijers, and it's too big to find anything there. Dennis took me once, but he yelled at me because I tried to drive the motorized shopping cart, and I knocked over the Mountain Dew display. That's how they'd found the tumor. A shadow passed over my eyes from left to right when I was driving, and I plowed my red Taurus station wagon into another car. That was the last time I drove, except for that shopping cart at Meijers. They were so mad at me. I just wish I could drive. I'm not going back to Meijers in this lifetime. Elisa is late as usual; she never comes when she says she is going to. She always has something more important to do, and she knows I have to wait for her. I looked at the last two photos in the album. One was of me when I was twenty-eight years old with my sixth child on my lap and the rest of the girls gathered around in their little sailor dresses. Elisa is on her father's lap. Even when she was small, she preferred him to me.

When the kids were really bad, I used to line them up oldest to youngest and give them one belt with the wooden flute. But Frankie never got it because Elisa would swirl around and grab the flute with her hand and fix me with a glare that scared me. But I completely lost control only once, and Dennis pulled me off of her before anything really bad happened. I wrote an apology letter to them. I said I was sorry I got angry last night, and then we never spoke of it, but Elisa slumped around the house in a long-sleeved turtleneck for days and flinched every time I came near her. Things were never the same with Dennis. That was the beginning of the end, when Elisa and Dennis both turned their backs on me. He should have taken my side. Elisa has never listened to or obeyed me.

The last picture in the album was the Glamour Shots one I gave all the girls and Dennis. I'd turned fifty, and I wanted to do something special. It had been at least six years since Dennis had touched me, and I knew we couldn't last much longer like this. So I went to Glamour Shots with my purple blazer, my paisley scarf, and makeup just so. By the time the Glamour Shots people were done with me, I was showing a pale shoulder, my hair was all tousled, and my lips were so shiny they glimmered.

Elisa, just home for a visit from college, took one look at my bare shoulder and recoiled, as if I'd shown her a naked picture. She didn't say anything and left soon after. She didn't hug me or say goodbye, and then she walked to the bus station by herself.

When I gave the picture to Dennis, he barely glanced at it before he said, "That's a nice picture," then tried to hand it back to me. I knew then it was too late to keep my marriage together.

That's when I met Sherie; then Lynnie, my first true love; then Ana; then Renee, my soulmate whose kids broke us up; and then Ailene, who won't even speak to me. So I have to wait for Elisa; at least she's not as selfish as Teresa, my oldest. Teresa comes over with one hand open for money and the other clutching a cigarette. Depending on her mood and the state of my pocketbook, she'll have time for me, and I won't have to be alone. Elisa won't even come over when Teresa is here, so I have to juggle, and most of the time Teresa wins. Elisa stays away.

Today I have presents: two porcelain dolls from the CVS Pharmacy after-Christmas sale wrapped up for Nereida and Maria. I've been telling Elisa about the presents since Three Kings Day. It's almost February, and she's finally here. The girls bound in and pounce on the presents and then on me as they hold up the dolls. "Thank you, Grandma!" shouts Nereida. Maria is reading the box. "Made in China," she announces.

"Do you like them, Elisa?"

"We'll find a place for them, Mom," she answers without enthusiasm.

The trip to the grocery store was a disaster for me. The three of them went to the elevator and waited impatiently, while I fumbled with my keys, my bag, and my cane. Downstairs they were always three steps ahead of me, and I had to wait in the cold while Elisa cleaned off the front passenger seat. She checked for messages on her cellphone and looked irritated when I asked for help with my seat belt. I just can't see out of that side of my head anymore, but she yanked at the seat belt impatiently. Why is Elisa always so angry?

"I can buy you some food with my Bridge Card, honey," I offered. "You know I don't eat very much. The medicine upsets my stomach."

Her back stiffened. "That's all right, Mom. Stock up on some dry goods."

I really did have money on my Bridge Card. "How about some cookies?" I knew she loved molasses cookies. Nereida was talking to her and playing with her mossy green purse.

"No, Mom, no thanks." She didn't even pretend to hide her irritation this time.

I taught my girls to give and to receive, and I'll never understand Elisa's prickly attitude. I waited for her to check out, then slipped the cookies onto the counter. I caught up to them in the parking lot, holding the bags in my right arm, balancing without my cane, and slipped the cookies into her bag. Maria caught me.

"Look, Mom! Grandma gave us some cookies!"

The girls ruined the surprise, but I still waited for Elisa's reaction. She didn't say anything. Instead she steered me out of the path of an approaching car and shouted at the girls, who were bounding ahead. She clipped us into our seats and turned on the radio.

My daughter is beautiful, and she won't let me near her.

Independence Day—Young Adulthood: The 1990s

The Cadet

Independence Day

Stealing

El Salvador, Central America

Driving to El Salvador
with Hector and Domingo

You Belong Here

The Cadet

Elisa, 1983

It was signing day for the Army ROTC unit at the University of Michigan. Four years of tuition in exchange for an all-expenses trip to a base in the rural South and then deployment to South Korea or the Middle East. I begged my parents one last time to fill out the financial aid forms, but they waved me off.

"We don't have the taxes," Mom answered, "Besides, you have the Army scholarship like your sister Darcy. Hurry up and go sign." I knew I would have to go and put on the face that says: "I want to be all I can be." The performance was required in my family. I thought again of the high school journalism conference, when afterward the presenter from *USA Today* had singled me out.

"You ask the most amazing questions," he said. "Have you thought of going into journalism? You'd be great." He handed me a card and said, "Let me know when you get to college."

I wouldn't know until years later that it was an invitation for something called an internship. I'd kept that card and looked at it until it was worn through and unreadable.

Mother had said the Army was looking for cadets and that's what I should do.

"I'm going to be able to tell people that I have another soldier in the family." Her smile almost reached her eyes. I knew I'd be taking the bus up to the university, and I would sign the papers, and I would be an Army soldier, and everyone would be very happy.

It was a humid Michigan summer day, and the air wavered with heat. The crumbling castlelike facade of North Hall, home of the ROTC, looked like a direct deposit from the *Rocky Horror Picture Show*. I faltered up the crumbling stone steps and plucked a clover growing between the cracks, crunching down on the sweet white flower. A North Campus-bound bus picked up a bearded man with a backpack. I followed its progress as it pointed toward the river and the brand-new dorms where the engineers lived and studied. It would for sure be nice to take a bus ride up there, walk around, visit the historical library. But I knew there was no more time for exploration. My path was set.

I opened the heavy wooden doors to a panel of men in uniform sitting around a long table. They stopped talking and shuffling papers when I entered the room and stood before them. The Army ROTC officers knew my sister Darcy was a top student. I wasn't a top student. I'd been coached.

"Don't tell them about your problems in high school. Don't ever say that," Mom said. I grimaced, trying to remember her instructions.

"Good afternoon," I said, then waited for them to speak. I cast around looking for a friendly face. Captain Krekkler had a high forehead and a wandering eye. I focused on the eye that wasn't moving around.

"Good afternoon," he returned. "So we've looked over your materials, and all is in order." He held out a stack of papers, my application, I supposed. "Can you tell us a little about why you want to be part of the US Army?"

I saw the campus through the window behind the men: brick dorm buildings and an expanse of green lawn, so different from so much of Detroit.

"I want to serve my country," I said. I'd practiced this in front of a mirror. "We believe that in my family." I thought of my sister, my cousins, my aunt and uncle, with their blue uniforms, green uniforms, stripes and gold buttons, strange and crisp robots in costume, marching in perfect cadence. "I'm prepared to serve." I imagined myself bending down, putting on combat boots, and following my older sister. It was the only way out of Detroit. I tried not to think of my little sister, Frankie. She was still in Detroit and probably would live with Mom and Dad forever; they'd never let her go to art school. But not me.

"Cadet Sinnett?" I looked up. Captain Krekkler was holding out a pen. I knew I had to sign, but I felt my throat closing. I stepped forward and held out my hand.

Independence Day

Elisa, 1985

"Today is my last day in Detroit for the rest of my life," I told myself. I was on my coffee break at the Detroit Golf Club, and I had just told Dominic and Russell that I was turning in my uniforms, quitting, and moving to West Virginia with my boyfriend, Paul, to work as a Catholic lay missionary.

"We're going to build houses with this nun in Appalachia," I said.

"Elisa, you're fucking crazy." Dominic's eyes glinted. He had used the same look on me when I told him my Ouija board story. Our conversations about religion never accomplished anything; I didn't think he believed in God, and he had laughed when I told him, "The Ouija board is the tool of the devil."

"Listen," Russell added, "it's just that we're going to get laid off in four weeks. We're all going to get unemployment. Everyone on the grounds crew. You too."

I'd never gotten laid off before. I'd always had a job, so if the management at the golf course was going to fire me, then I was going to quit first—I couldn't wait until after Halloween to start my life. The mornings were already getting crisper, and I had to wear a jacket over my uniform. I loved my blue pants, my steel-toed boots, and my work shirt that said ELISA over the left pocket. I didn't want to turn them in.

"You don't have to, Elisa," said Dominic. "Just one more month of being the oppressed workers, toiling for the capitalist pigs, and we all get to sit around and smoke all day if we want to."

Russell laughed. "Elisa, you get the job back in March. We're just laid off for the winter." My parents didn't work for the union, and they never got any time off. I felt panic at the thought of not working all the time, even though we had all been working twelve-hour shifts every weekend day since May. It was in my blood, or maybe just in my brain, to keep moving at all costs.

"Elisa, you can relax, you know." Was Dominic a mind reader too?

When he turned his blue eyes on me, I was ready to agree with almost anything. His chest was so thick, I wanted to grab him and hold on. He seemed steady, solid. But then he started with politics, and it ended with him saying something like, "So, Elisa, we should get high together." Or, "Elisa, we should really sleep together."

So where did Dominic think we were going to end up with his plan? And why did Dominic get "the look" in his eyes when I told him about my fiancé, Paul?

"So why do you think he's willing to wait for marriage, Elisa?"

I looked at Dominic like he didn't hear what I was saying.

"We're Catholic," I said. "We want to do the right thing."

"So does he kiss you? Tell you he can't wait for that special day so he can..." I put my hand out. I noticed that the hair on my arms was bleached blond, and my freckles had migrated into one giant constellation.

"Stop," I said. "It's none of your business."

"So when's your magical day?" He bent down to tie his boot, but his jaw was clenched.

"Um, we haven't set a date," I said. "I think God is calling us to be of service in Appalachia." I washed out my coffee cup with a grayish-looking rag and placed the cup on the drying rack with the rest of the dishes in the dull metal industrial sink. I turned toward Dominic. The break was almost over.

"Elisa, you don't have to believe that shit. You have a perfectly good job, enough money to do what you want." Dominic opened a door in my head, like something was shining a light on me. I couldn't tell if I was terrified or in love. No one had ever spoken to me like that. I felt a weight lifting from my chest; I stepped toward him, then stepped closer. He was seated, his legs splayed, his pose casual, but his eyes never left mine. I felt like I was at the crest of the Chandler Park hill on my bicycle, about to kick off and ride down, no hands on the handlebars. I stepped into the V of his legs.

"Dominic," I began. I didn't know what I was going to say. "God's not something that you can just throw out." I wanted an answer that I could live with that started with me taking one more step into his arms. But then Russell came in, clearing his throat loudly and clanking his cup into the sink.

"Your dad's looking for you, Dominic." He glanced at me. "Elisa, you're supposed to get the red cart and follow Archiem." The moment passed.

I couldn't take a chance with Dominic. At home, Mom still screamed at Dad, but Dad had checked out, staring at his computer screen. I was next in the line of fire, and Dad already had dibs on the withdrawal strategy. Mom followed me around and needled me until I cleaned out the furnace room and the laundry room under her supervision.

"Elisa. Get this box. Hold it. Wait. Somebody's got to take responsibility for this house. Put it up there. No. Put the paint in here. No. Leave it out. Look at the peeling paint. Get the scraper. Somebody's got to care about what happens in this house."

I needed to get away, to get some perspective. I'd hardly been anywhere except for Canada and Detroit. That's why I was leaving Detroit with Paul. Paul believed in God, and after we went on our mission, we'd be married. It was all planned.

"You don't live here anymore," Mom said. "You're supposed to be independent. You're the one that gave up the Army scholarship." I knew how to arm a Claymore mine. I could rappel down the dentistry building at the UM Ann Arbor campus. I could take apart an M-16 and put it back together in two minutes. I could do sixty-nine sit ups in a minute, and I could run three miles without stopping or throwing up. But none of these skills seemed to be helping me right then. When one of the sergeants in the ROTC had made some kind of clerical error and we had to sign the Army paperwork again, two of us had considered it a lucky escape.

Being unable to continue at college was an unfortunate side effect. I lost my chance when I defied Mother and didn't do all the paperwork to keep the Army scholarship. I wanted to ask my Ouija board for help, but defying Mom and God at the same time seemed dangerous. I burned the Ouija board. I wanted to ask what I could do. What course of action would be best?

1. Smoking pot with Dominic in somebody's basement and talking about the capitalist oppressors.

2. Leaving with Paul.

3. Getting unemployment.

4. Losing my virginity to a sixty-year-old golfer and getting him to pay for college in exchange for sexual favors.

Drug addicts smoked weed. Lazy people took unemployment, and I was not lazy. I couldn't afford college, and I turned down Mr. Well's offer to pay for college by going off with him in his Cadillac. He loved that I was a virgin. I don't know why I told him; maybe I thought reminding him that he was married and I was a virgin would politely send him away. Instead, he asked me to go for a ride in the golf cart with him.

"Elisa, I want you to think about college," he said. His cart skirted the sand trap and went out into the rough, in the no-man's land by the far corner of the golf course.

"Of course. I mean. I was at college. I lost my scholarship." It was the end of summer with the smell of fresh cut grass in the air.

"There are other ways," he said. "I could help." He moved closer.

"Mr. Wells, I can't do that," I whispered.

Shame engulfed me when I punched the clock that day. Dominic was there; he'd been waiting for me.

"Elisa, what's up?" he said, moving closer. "I couldn't stop thinking about earlier, in the break room." He reached for the back of my neck, pulled my face toward him. "I think this is what was about to happen this morning."

"Fuck off! Don't try to kiss me! I'm leaving tomorrow. That's it!" I pushed past him and walked toward the pool house with quick strides. My insides wilted when I saw the young people my age lounging by the pool. They looked like paper doll caricatures of their mothers with floppy straw hats, zinc oxide on their noses, and frothy drinks held aloft. One spoke to me as I connected the hose and uncoiled it.

"You missed one. Come here, finish your job!" I pretended not to hear her and ducked around the corner of the massive red brick clubhouse and headed straight out the second fairway at a half-trot, then running for Stevie Wonder's pink house like a beacon. I crossed through his backyard and walked onto the facing street. Turning right, toward 7 Mile, I unbuttoned my blue work shirt, slung it over my shoulder, and wiped my sweaty hands on my white T-shirt. I was halfway home. I willed myself not to think about Dominic. I felt bad about the flowers and leaving the hose running.

Who was I kidding? I really, really wanted to climb into Dominic's car and start driving, down Woodward until the river, then across the Ambassador Bridge to Canada, then up the lakeshore, north and north until all we could see was trees and stars, and we would find a small cabin in a birch grove. I would lay my head against his chest and cry for an hour in relief, that I almost missed this forever. I almost didn't pick him. Then we would take off all our clothes in the firelight, and my hands and lips would be free to do what I'd been thinking about for weeks, but there were no promises, none at all. I was afraid. I was afraid of all the things I wanted. It was bad to grow up around rich people. It made me want their life, even if I hated them, and they made my life seem smaller. It was not like I ever wanted to be friends with the girls from grade school who lived along the golf course anyway. But I didn't think I'd end up with their grandpa's cigar breath whispering insistent and horrible proposals in my ear.

I won't lie. I wanted to stop worrying about money all together. I could move out of my house tonight, but just thinking about Mr. Wells's pleading and rheumy eyes put an end to that line of thought. Dominic was dangerous; my brain stopped working when I was around him. Paul and I believed the same things, dreamed the same future. I didn't have a month to wait around until I was laid off. I had today, and I had to leave while I was still sure of Paul, before I let anybody derail me.

*

So today is the day, I thought. This is the day that the Lord has made. That was a song stuck in my head. It was six o'clock in the morning, and I sat on the front porch with my Stroh's beer case packed with clothes, four peanut butter-and-jelly sandwiches, two apples, a jar of water, and a sleeping bag. I waited for Paul to show up in the black GMC Jimmy 4x4 I had bought, placing his name on the title because he lived out in the suburbs by the airport, and everything was so far away. Paul, like many suburbanites, refused to come into Detroit after dark, so I didn't see him very often. He needed the truck more than I did; I could walk to work at the club. It was only 1½ miles if I walked down the wide, cool streets of my neighborhood, then down Fairway Drive, and cut through the backyard of Stevie Wonder's pink house, then across the golf course.

Detroit has always been so beautiful, but it's choked off by suburbs sliced into narrow strips by mile roads serving as overcrowded, two-lane highways with a thousand cars honking and slamming on the brakes. A person had to know exactly where they were going because there were never any landmarks in the suburbs, except for the giant tire on I-94. Even the sailors on the ocean had stars back in the Viking days to steer their ships. Suburbanites lived in a state of permanent twilight created by street after street of bungalows casting a wash of light that erased the stars. I could still see the stars in the early morning when I walked out on the golf course. I wondered what they would be like in West Virginia.

I could hear the truck coming up the street, the sound of my new life, like wheels turning, like music. I was already on my feet, carrying my beer case and trying to wrench open the hatch in the back of the truck.

"Hi, babe." Paul had to lean down to kiss me. I always kissed the dimple in the middle of his chin. He looked like the son of a golfer. I think he was, but his parents couldn't afford to golf where I worked. They wouldn't dream of coming into Detroit and were against us hooking up in the first place. Where I lived in Detroit, the houses were large and stately, made of stone and brick, and only a few blocks to Palmer Woods with its mansion-lined streets built by the founders of the auto companies. The Detroit Golf Club was for the auto company executives, not for the line workers like Paul's family who lived in tract houses out in the suburbs and could barely afford a set of golf clubs. Paul's family wouldn't dream of going anywhere inside the city limits. Sometimes I believed Paul imagined himself above me, although both of us were broke and had nowhere to go, even if our parents did have some version of the American dream working out for them.

"Ready for Appalachia?" I faked what I hoped was a southern accent and, with a final twist, turned the metal handle on the back window and stuffed my sleeping bag and beer case in.

"Yes, ma'am," he imitated me.

We drove down 6 Mile toward the freeway and Appalachia. We were going to try out the Catholic version of Habitat for Humanity.

The first leg was easy. We rumbled down I-75 south toward Toledo, Ohio, sixty miles away, famous for being in a John Denver song called "Saturday Night in Toledo, Ohio." The lyrics made it sound like it was a very boring place

I spread the map out on my lap. I was excellent at this because land navigation was one of the military science classes I aced. The rain started, hard, in Marietta, Ohio. By that time of the afternoon, we should have been a little closer to our destination of Lick Fork, West Virginia, but we forgot to turn off in Toledo and spent the better part of the early afternoon discovering the long way through Columbus, Ohio, which we also learned had a beltway, like Washington, DC. A person could keep circling the city and never find the right freeway. I saw the sign to the OSU stadium at least three times, and then we had to stop for gas. I think the truck was running a little hot, but I didn't say anything to Paul; he didn't like me to talk when he was trying to see the road.

I wanted to head back to Marietta and find a place to wait out the rain. It was five o'clock and already dark with the rain falling and the storm clouds pluming up in giant towering stacks. It was going to be dark for real pretty soon. Looking at the map, there wasn't much in the way of cities once you got into West Virginia, and most of the roads were of the skinny kind, not the fat red ones I liked to see that indicated actual highways. Marietta was the last thing on the map that looked bigger than a tiny white dot.

"Look, Paul, I don't think we're going to make it today." I was hesitant. I didn't want to piss him off while he was driving. "Marietta is only about ten miles back. We could stop; get something to eat. Find a place to sleep, you know."

"Elisa, I'm trying to drive." He squinted at the road between the windshield wipers looking for the clear patch so he could drive. *The Best of Bread* played on the cassette player. We'd listened to that tape three times already, driving around Columbus, Ohio. I knew we wouldn't be driving back to Marietta.

All my life I had lived below sea level in a city that had wide streets, green trees, and bright lights. The neon lights in Marietta had felt soothing at least: yellow M's shining bright in the dark gray sky, HOTEL $29 for a double bed, blue Marathon gas signs. I wanted to stop and stay in all the lights, not this dark highway, rainy and slippery, that rolled up and out into the darkness. The foothills of the Appalachias were higher now, closer together. This highway through West Virginia didn't feel like home. Paul drove down into a valley and through a huge puddle, crawling over the highway. I heard the sluice of the wheels driving through deep water, and then we started to hydroplane, and the tread-poor wheels of the Jimmy tried to gain purchase on the other side of the dip. Paul had a cool head, at least in the moment; he didn't try to wildly steer, and we made it to the other side.

"See?" He smirked at me, a triumphant look on his face.

"Did you turn off the radio?" I asked him. At the same moment, the headlights started to dim.

"Oh shit!" Paul tried to pull over.

The first exit in fifty miles loomed like a miracle of loaves and fishes. I punched at the radio buttons, everything, even the defroster. The truck chugged and lurched up the ramp and slid through the stop sign, over a two-lane road, and into a parking lot of a one-story building with a crooked sign: two eggs, bacon, coffee: Breakfast Special: 99 cents. We saw the boarded-up windows at the same time.

Paul made a sound. I stayed very quiet. At least we weren't on the highway.

My heart was still beating fast, and I could see Paul's knuckles gripping the steering wheel, not letting go. The sound of rain drummed on the roof of the Jimmy. I willed Paul not to try to start the car. For a moment, the creepy, far-away feeling was gone. There was something peaceful about being off the freeway; the mountains had a fresh smell of wet pine needles. And even though we were in the parking lot of a closed-up diner in West Virginia, we weren't in Detroit, and nobody knew where we were. It was a giddy feeling. Detroit was a glittery necklace that had disappeared in the mist like a mythical place, far, far away. I stretched my arms over my head and then unclipped my seat belt, reached into the glove box, and pulled out two Marlboro Lights and the lighter. Nicotine was manna from heaven at this point, better than food. My nerves were already calming at the red glow of the cigarettes, the horror story that was unspooling in my mind on hold. Paul let go of the steering wheel and grabbed his smoke. He whooshed a big exhale of breath, unclipped his seat belt, and pushed his seat back.

"Thanks, Elisa." Paul turned. "I think this is just what I needed." He seemed glad that I wasn't going to bring up any recriminations about not turning back and going to Marietta. We didn't have money anyway to stay at hotels. The rain continued to drum steadily on the roof, and the temperature was dropping. "You got anything to eat?" There were two apples left and half a jar of water. Paul pulled some fuzzy beef jerky sticks out of his shirt pocket. I leaned into the seat, noticing how his flannel squared over his wide shoulders. He rubbed his thumb over his cleft chin as he smoked. The cross, made of two nails, was hidden under his shirt. His smell was pure male, musky, smoky. I leaned my head on him for a minute before we made a poor supper, staring out the windows and craning our necks to see if any cars were passing. The road was quiet. I guess West Virginians know when to keep their cars off the road. I squinted, trying to read the map by the lighter light.

"I think we're right here." I pointed at a vast expanse of green bumps with no comforting towns in bold black letters.

"I'm sorry, Elisa. We're not going to get any help before morning." Paul sounded more like himself for the first time since we left Marietta and drove into the downpour. "Let's make a run for it."

We stepped out in the rain and made a dash to the back of the truck. Paul boosted me up, then climbed into the covered truck bed. We could already see our breaths. We dried off with a clean shop rag, climbed into our sleeping bags, and turned toward each other, two cocoons facing each other, breathing each other's air, waiting for morning.

Stealing

Elisa, 1986

In college, I wasn't a pretty drunk. I suppose I only think I am now. There is no sitcom that my life remotely resembles. Movie? Maybe *Girl, Interrupted*. Book? *Woman on the Edge of Time*. But I'm not the heroine who eventually makes it out of the insane asylum. I'm the one who doesn't. The unsympathetic character. No, not the defiant and heroic one who dies, the other one. The side character. The crazy, overlooked one. That's me.

Put her in this story. The one with the Army coat that's too long, pant cuffs too frayed, shoes scuffed. The wrong kind. She works at the Village Corner in Ann Arbor, the VC. Where the hipsters work. She isn't one. They are proud of their hip status and their hip jobs. She's also a university student like them, but they disregard her, rebuff her small overtures of friendship while refilling the beer cooler. She heard two of them talking about something called the US/El Salvador Sister City project. Travel—that was the good part of the Army scholarship. "That sounds interesting." She didn't know what else to say, but they had turned away, one of them had mumbled something that sounded like "baby killer." But that couldn't be right. She'd give it a week, try again. She had always gotten along well with people she worked with. How hard could it be to find some people to party with?

This time, the skinny one, Kate, and the dude with the long blond hair are standing by the time clock. She hears them say "party," "open," "keg," "after work." She walks up to them, a smile on her face. They stop talking, greet her in polite, tinny voices, start talking again after she punches out. If she told them she was from Detroit, what would they say? This era comes during the pre-hipster invasion of Detroit, so it wouldn't get her anything. They'd just freak out.

She gets drunk by herself, later, in the cheapest way possible, then does what she always does; she starts walking, prowling the streets of Ann Arbor. She doesn't have anywhere to go, but constant movement helps. She staggers back into the Village Corner, chewing on an old candy cane, and asks to use the employee bathroom. The story she blurts out is that she's meeting her boyfriend at a party; she's been studying. The night crew waves her on, heads already turned away. She passes aisles of candy in the dark storage area. On her way back through, she stuffs the pockets of her father's Army jacket with Laffy Taffys and Charms bubble gum pops. She spends the rest of the evening walking and trying to taste sweetness, wishing there was something bigger she could steal.

El Salvador, Central America

Elisa, 1990

It was the farthest I had been from Detroit in my life. I drove there. It took nine days. I really want to say, "I drove to El Salvador" because it makes me sound like a decisive person. Truth was, I'd lost my Army scholarship, and I'd used up all my unemployment checks. I had no idea on how to find a new job. I'd been working with my dad and his sister stuffing envelopes and doing billing for the car companies, but they had just filed for bankruptcy.

I didn't drive by myself to Central America. I went with my Salvadoran boyfriend, Oswaldo, who was my *novio* because my Spanish was so bad that I had agreed to be his girlfriend before I knew what he was saying, and by the time I had figured it out, it seemed rude to set him straight. Besides there was two feet of dirty snow piling up outside my apartment, and Mingo, Oswaldo's brother-in-law, was in town. He wanted us to drive to El Salvador with him. Mingo's best friend, Rudy, was in a teacher's union and was in some kind of trouble with the Salvadoran government.

Our job, Mingo explained, would be easy. "See, we drive to El Salvador, and we pick up Rudy and his family. On the way back, Elisa, you get to drive." I stared at him, head tilted.

"We get out of the car before we get up to the checkpoints. You talk to the immigration officers at the Casitas in Mexico, and we run around them. You drive a mile or two, and you pick us up." Mingo leaned back with his arms crossed, as if that explained everything.

"Um," I thought I heard him right, "and that would make me..."

"*Una coyote*!" Oswaldo seemed to like the idea.

Bringing people over the border illegally. I could get arrested.

I walked over to the window and looked out the blinds, looked out at Detroit. It was gray and cold. I was already imagining El Salvador as a dark green jewel in a pirate movie: dangerous, sparkly, and far, far away.

"Okay." I faced Oswaldo and Mingo. "I'll do it."

We drove to El Salvador. It took us nine days. Two of the days were spent in a scary small town near Little Rock, Arkansas, getting a new alternator for Mingo's 1985 silver-tone Grand Am. Another day was spent as guests of the Guatemalan army beside the Pan-American Highway in a small jail. They locked me alone in the cell next to one with about twenty- five shirtless men, impassive, standing, waiting. None of them even looked my way, not even Oswaldo or Mingo. I wasn't sure what taboo was suddenly in place, but I knew then that I would not be a modern-day driver for the Underground Railroad, bringing death squad escapees to freedom. It was a farce, and I hated myself for a moment. The Guatemalan soldiers were younger than me, but they had machine guns, and I was afraid of them. It wasn't until they found my stash of American Express Travelers Cheques in my Kotex box that they finally cleared us.

Three days after we made it to Oswaldo's house, Mingo took a joyride and totaled his car off the side of a steep hill on the incline between San Pedro Nonualco and San Emigdio el Tablon. So we were out of money and without transport.

Oswaldo's father spent his days sleeping on the concrete ledge outside their house. His mother, Esperanza, walked to church every morning, pinch faced and wearing a handkerchief on her head. His little sister, Yesenia, brought Mingo cups of brown sugar lemonade and slices of mango while he sat nursing his broken ribs and smashed-up face. Oswaldo stood outside the playground at the secondary school and tried to talk to girls in the green skirts and white socks through the playground fence. I went and sat on the steps of the mayor's office/library/town hall and was surrounded by eight-year-olds wanting me to say something in English. I ended up learning a lot of Spanish, but the children did not believe that I came from a place where the days were sometimes almost sixteen hours long. Their days were always close to twelve hours. Night and day, breathing in and out in the slow rhythm of this green and verdant place.

I still had my American passport, and after three months I got up enough courage to call my sister Darcy and ask her to send me enough money to come back to the United States. I knew I was in for a lecture about dropping the Army scholarship and getting stuck in Central America. I do have an explanation for how these things always happen to me. I just have a lot of energy, you know? My family said this is the last time they're bailing me out. I was headed back to Detroit to find a job. Maybe I could go back to school to become a teacher. It was time to go home.

Driving to El Salvador with Hector and Domingo

Wheatley, Arkansas, 1990

I never knew that I passed invisible in my own country
the double yellow lines of a two-lane highway leading me
to perhaps a cup of coffee
sitting down with hands clutching
a shiny brown mug
blowing steam with pursed lips.

We smile at the waitress
dressed in brown polyester, mousy hair.
"Hi, my name is Susan," welcomes her name tag.

But she doesn't smile back.

I look across the linoleum counter
and see that we are surrounded
by an army of men, dressed in checked shirts, caps,
talking of distances traveled in their rumbling trucks.

I no longer walk invisible
in my own country.
I travel today with two men,
that God has dressed in brown skin,
and a soft lilting language

that stands in contrast to their violent past
of Spanish conquistadores
and guerillas and soldiers
of a long civil war.

I speak their language too, and
inherit the violence.

It is within

and

it belongs to the waitress
in brown polyester
and the men in checked shirts.

In their eyes I see
Atlanta burning.

I hear them whistling "Dixie."

But it's not the song of a
bird skimming above a sunbaked field

or a young boy kicking up clods of dirt
bare feet sinking in fresh loam.

It is the death march of men;
hooded men in white.

I hear a drum pulsing loudly and
see a shadowy figure swinging from a tree.

The sweat is gathering on my palms.
I look up and see the waitress in the brown dress.
"Your bill," she says flatly.

I feel a prickling on my neck of curious stares
and feel the drum beat more urgently now.

I put three dollars on the counter
and we leave quickly.

I open the glass door, the night air
biting my flushed cheeks
And
dream of a world
without nations.

You Belong Here

Teresa, 1995

Teresa limped down the boardwalk in a short white dress, the uniform of the partygoer in the spring break haven of Myrtle Beach, South Carolina. Her clunky cork wedge sandals didn't get stuck in the cracks, but they were tied on, gladiator style, and her right foot was slipping. In the deepening twilight she could still pull off the look of a younger woman. Teresa took out her cellphone to call one of her girlfriends, to tell them about Joey's latest bullshit, but then put it back away. They weren't really her friends. They hadn't even left the bar with her when Joey had started calling her names.

"You fucking whore!" Joey had come up to their table at The Clam Shack bristling and wired on coke. At least he thought she looked good enough to get men's attention, but it was too much— his accusation that she was somehow fucking his cousin Tito, their roommate, and her friend Marissa, who was trying to get with Tito. What a soap opera.

"Yo! Joey! You're the one who's late. Don't you remember you told Tito to pick me and Marissa up?" Teresa could see he didn't remember his idea for all of them to meet up for drinks.

"Don't you tell me what I did." Joey's finger was in her face. "Or I'll..." He put out his fist.

Teresa covered her mouth, protecting the one chipped tooth he had put there the time he accused the pizza delivery guy of "sleeping with his girl." *God, what a jerk*, she thought.

"That's it, I'm out of here. Tito, you keep your cousin off of me. That's it, Joey!"

"Marissa, you coming?" Teresa hesitated, then saw Marissa gesture toward Tito, mouthing, "Sorry!"

She had scraped her white straw purse from the table and sashayed out.

Teresa turned down the boardwalk, away from the tourist strip. She'd left Joey before, but since he controlled the money, she'd never gotten very far. Maybe she should try to get her own job, not just being at Joey's beck and call the minute she ran out of cash.

She thought her best bet would be to get a job at a bar; maybe she should find the spot—what was it—the SandBar? That's where the businessmen liked to hang out. That sounded prosperous. Teresa was surprised how far down the SandBar was, almost to the edge of the red-light district. She was already a little tipsy when she pushed through the door and her ankle turned, but a tanned man in a light suit caught her by the elbow.

"Are you okay? Can I buy you a drink?"

My luck must be changing, she thought.

Maybe she wasn't meant to work, and having a boyfriend who had some money could be good.

"Oh, sure," she said. "How about a Bacardi and Diet Coke?"

Teresa tottered over to the ladies room, patted at her strawberry blond hair, undid another button so her lace bra showed a little bit, and rejoined her date.

"So what's your name?"

"You can call me Jonah." He took a sip of beer.

"Oh, Bacardi hits the spot. You should try it."

"Maybe I will," he said, not looking at her drink, but down at the lace peeping out of her blouse.

She leaned in to show her interest, licked her lips, and sucked on her straw. His suit was synthetic, his face a little too tan. A salesman maybe? He started to jiggle his leg, antsy, his eyes flicking over to the basketball game on TV.

"So you're done with your drink? Ready to get going?"

Teresa hesitated.

"Do I pay you up front, or after...?" He drew out the last word, not finishing the sentence.

"What?"

"For your, you know, services." His finger reached out, traced a line down her cheek, and rested between her breasts.

"Oh." That was why her ex-bosses came over here; she felt sick. She scanned the bar with new eyes. There were at least three older-looking businessmen with younger women showing skin or lace or both.

"Sure, I'll be right back." She stumbled out the side door and hurried away, listening for footsteps. *How could I have missed the clues?*

Teresa flagged a cab and gave an address on a side of town she had hoped to never see again. The Mai Tai was off the beaten track; crowded, but not with tourists and rich kids on break. It was as far from the boardwalk as she could be and still be in Myrtle Beach.

Her eyes scanned the crowd. She knew these people—the professional partiers, men and women in year-round tans, bronzed and raspy voiced from smoking and late nights. She pulled up to the bar and ordered a Bacardi and Diet Coke; no need to get fat. The bartender was a little older, maybe by five or six years, but down here where the sun never stopped shining, the woman was paying for it in wrinkles. Teresa saw her talking to an older, light-skinned man, gray just touching his temples. Teresa caught his eye; he winked, and she smiled back at him.

"What can I get you, sweetheart?" he asked, then, "Tammy, get her another Bacardi and Diet Coke." The older woman nearly slammed the drink down and gave Teresa a hard look.

"I've got this one, Tammy," he said, staring at the bartender until she stomped to the other end of the bar.

Teresa saw that she had a chance. He was either the manager or, better yet, the owner. "I used to tend bar. I know a lot about things that taste really good when combined," she said and licked her lips. She knew she had a job when she saw him swallow. At the end of a long night, she was pleased to witness a scene that took place at the far end of the bar. It ended with the older bartender ripping off her apron in fury and slamming out. Teresa knew her time had arrived. She would follow him upstairs, would follow him anywhere.

*

That's how the years slid by, the whole tenor of her life changed by one night and one person. There is Jerry's bar, there is Jerry's bed, and there is the beach. Some mornings it was hard to get out of bed, and she needed a few shots of whiskey to get her going; her stomach burned. But then she'd make it out to the beach, light up a cigarette, and hang out. She would tell anyone who asked, "Life is good."

She didn't make a plan to go back to Detroit until two things happened, and both on the same night. The first was a phone call from her little sister. Elisa called every few months to pass on family gossip or to try to get her to come home.

"Teresa, I have to tell you something....Dad..."

Teresa had a moment of fear. Had something happened to Dad?

"I heard Dad and Mom talking," she continued. "And Dad's been acting really freaky. I think you really should come home."

"Elisa, what? What's going on with Dad? And why are you calling me about it?"

Elisa paused. "Dad had an eye operation. They poked his eye with a needle, and when he came home, he was still high on whatever they gave him at the hospital. Teresa, Dad was crying. He said you were his real daughter, no matter what Mom did in the past, and that he missed you. I'm not lying."

It was Teresa's turn to be silent a moment. "It's not like Dad ever really knows what's going on. I don't believe you."

"Teresa...Just come home for Christmas. You'll see."

Teresa sipped on Bacardi and Diet Cokes, one after another, asking Elisa questions until she was hyped up on the caffeine and buzzed. But the details didn't matter. Dad must have always known that Mom had been afraid to tell the truth. About who Teresa's real dad was. About Teresa being attacked that night back in high school when he hadn't done anything to protect her. Dad never cried. Maybe this news from Elisa was as good as an apology as she was going to get from him. Maybe it was time. She just needed a sign.

Teresa took a taxi instead of riding her bike into work, but she was two hours late anyway. She weaved up to the bar and plastered her game-day face on, but in her place at the till was one of the younger waitresses. Teresa stared at the girl; was her name Jeanette?

"Thanks for covering for me, Jeanette." She took a stab at the girl's name with more bravado than she felt. "I've got it now." Teresa moved to step behind the bar, but then Jerry materialized.

"I don't think so, Teresa." He stopped her.

And then she realized paybacks are a bitch, and she should have known that there was no such thing as firm ground beneath her feet.

"I think you better get your shit out of Jerry's place." Jeanette walked to the end of the bar and reached into the back room. "Here." She shoved Teresa's flowered suitcase and her gym bag at her. "Take your shit." Twenty-five years in the same place, and she could carry her belongings in two hands, a permanent refugee, still looking for a home country.

*

The air was sparkly as she boarded her bus for the 800-mile journey to Detroit. The joint she smoked to calm herself down must have been laced with something; the trip came on in waves, each a little stronger. Teresa knew before long she would start hearing and seeing things. In the past, whenever she started to trip, she tried to hang onto reality. She'd reconstruct events, sometimes memories or a list of meals she enjoyed. Huge swaths of time were gone, but then an image would come with complete clarity like a camera zooming in on a single baby shoe during news coverage of a tornado's aftermath.

She remembered Dad sitting at the round, glass-topped table on the postcard-sized back patio on the outskirts of Myrtle Beach. Dad and his buddies from the old parish had driven down together from Detroit in a yellow Ford Econoline van for a guys-only fishing trip. He left his hotel by the pier and came inland to see her for a night. He was speaking in a low, urgent tone so her boyfriend, Joey, and his cousin wouldn't hear.

"These people are dangerous Teresa. You need to come home."

She leaned her head against the bus window, the glass cool on her forehead. She heard Dad's voice echoing in her head, then shifting to a different voice, the one she'd heard since she was a little girl. *Get out! Get out!* She closed her eyes and did something that she hadn't done in years. It wasn't exactly a prayer—she didn't even remember the words to prayers anymore; it was a memory, and she held onto it. It was back at the Stansbury house in Detroit. She'd fallen off her bike, and arms were holding her, a low voice was soothing her. She knew then that the whole time it had been Dad. And then the voice in her head changed. It was Dad's voice saying, "Come home, come home, come home."

There was someone waiting for her in Detroit, if she made it. She slept, the wheels of the bus pointing toward Detroit, Dad's voice the North Star.

The Greyhound bus neared the top of the Rouge River Bridge through the Delray section of Detroit. To her left was the Marathon Oil refinery, and to her right, inky plumes of greenish smoke rose from Zug Island. Her heart was racing, and her face was covered in beads of sweat. Her real dad, not her phantom bio family. Her real dad and the family that raised her wanted Teresa to come home.

It was her last chance, and it was the last place she wanted to be, but when the bus made it over the freeway bridge and she saw the downtown Detroit skyline and the Ambassador Bridge to Canada, she realized the air had lost its threatening sheen. She could breathe again.

Elegy for Our Home in Detroit: Y2K

Cesar and the Glass Slipper

No Organic Allowed

Water

Prayer Requests

Something You Build: Detroit

Mother, We Were So Close
When You Were Choking Me

"Bye, Mama"

Elegy for Our Home in Detroit

Cesar and the Glass Slipper

Elisa and Cesar, 1996

I'll tell you exactly how I met the girls' dad and everything that transpired. I was at a Mexican-Irish bar on a Tuesday night, because I was Irish and my best friend was Mexican, and we had a running joke about it. Lorena wanted to go out because she was pissed off about something, probably the guy that was ignoring her in favor of the Latina Entrepreneur. I was jumping up and down on my mini trampoline because I was pissed off at Isabella and her fake stalking story. She convinced Dr. Villanova to send her to work in my nice calm school on the far west side, and I got transferred to her middle school where a death curse was making its way through the building like an Old Testament Bible story. So far the history teacher's wife had hung herself while she was at work, the custodian's green-eyed son had been murdered, and a little boy had split his skull while hanging out the school bus window. The principal's blood disease and the teacher dropping dead of a heart attack in the middle of a grammar lesson hadn't happened yet, but I was already a nervous wreck every time I went to school, wondering, *who's next?*

So when my bestie Lorena called with the invitation to Sullivan's, I was in the shower in thirty seconds and waiting on the porch twelve minutes later. We bypassed the entrance to the

Ambassador Bridge to Canada and drove right into the bar's gravel parking lot.

I spotted Cesar the minute we walked in. Lorena warned me about Honduran dudes, but what could be more dangerous than working in a public school? Nothing. He had a short, stocky build and a round head, but so did I. It looked better on him. Cesar and I danced a Mexican polka, and if my baby timer wasn't going off then, it was a five-alarm fire by the end of the night.

I had to leave at midnight in a rush because I had to work the next morning. I accidentally dropped my shoe in the parking lot. Cesar tried to find me right away but had lost the keys to his truck sometime after his fifth beer. He had to wait until the next day to gather up his merry band of cousins and knock on all the doors in southwest Detroit holding my bright red Converse out and promising marriage. Because size seven is the most common women's shoe size, four hundred women had the same size foot as mine, but not one of them could untie the sailor knots I had learned while teaching crafts at the summer camp. I was the only one who could untie the laces. He was already down on one knee putting on the shoe, so he went ahead and proposed.

We had baby Maria in the fall, and Nereida two years later right around my birthday. We lived happily ever after.

No Organic Allowed

Elisa, Maria, and Nereida, 2000

"Mami! Look at me!" Maria, wearing a red snow suit, made a tiny snow angel on the sidewalk. "*Soy una angelita!*"

"Make another one, sweetie." I knelt in front of the baby's car seat, pulled on her glove, and ran my finger along Nereida's pale cheek. No hint of frostbite. Nereida's amber eyes regarded me without blinking.

I picked up my shovel and imagined we were upstairs, watching the snow from the living room. Being on the fourth floor blocked out most of the street noise, and the giant oak and its branches that grew almost up to the window transported us to a different place—softer and more forgiving than the one we lived in most of the time. Maybe I could make their world a safer one so they didn't have to constantly search out hiding places, looking for Narnia behind every closed door. Maybe they'd be the ones to get out of Detroit for real and escape the isolation and the constant scheming to survive.

I had to keep shoveling, and we had to go out. We'd been living on almond cookies, beans, and iced tea for two days, waiting for the fifteenth of the month to redeem the WIC coupons. The twelve inches of snow, Detroit's first blizzard of the new year, was just the latest obstacle.

"There. That should do it." The newly liberated Mazda's back was smashed in, and the insurance policy hadn't been paid in four months, but the 626 was all mine. After I clipped the girls into their seats, I pulled my sopping gloves off and searched my pockets for the screwdriver.

"There you are." I spent so much time with the little ones that I'd taken to speaking to objects. I did my special magic, twisting the screwdriver's flat head into the gaping ignition, and worked on my sound effects to get the girls to laugh.

"Vroom! Vroom!"

In the rearview mirror, Nereida's new Winnie-the-Pooh hat from Aunt Darcy, stationed in Korea, slipped down over one eye, but her other one was bright, and I could see her teeth as she laughed. Nereida loved the car.

I drove the car forward a few feet. "Just one second, *niñas*." I hopped out and pulled a yellow vinyl kitchen chair from the sidewalk into my cleaned-out parking spot. "I hope nobody moves you."

I fishtailed down Vinewood Street and took a left on Vernor Highway. The Mazda slid into the deep tire tracks as if lining up for a car wash. I patted my pocket for the WIC booklet. Because of this government program, I could buy milk, cereal, juice, cheese, beans, peanut butter, and some tuna fish for the girls. If cousin Carlo lifted more rice, green tea, and almond cookies from the Chinese restaurant where he worked, I calculated I could make it until my husband's next unemployment check. I'd believed Cesar when he said he was coming home for Navidad, but it was already the New Year, and he was still in Honduras. If it weren't for Carlo coming by every two weeks to help me fill out Cesar's unemployment papers and forge Cesar's signature, I'd have been in trouble.

Ryan's Foods's parking lot had been plowed, but the spaces were still covered in snow. I hustled in with the girls before the homeless woman by the door had a chance to beg from me. My arms were full, and I wasn't willing to set anybody down. Nereida's car seat took up almost the whole shopping cart, and

Maria's feet barely fit through the holes of the toddler seat. Maria helped with the WIC rules now: She pointed at the green Juicy Juice bottle with the apples on it and clapped. I navigated the aisles, pushing the cart with one hand, tucking food around Nereida, double-checking against the WIC brochure so I didn't miss a thing.

"Meat! Meat! Meat!" Maria chanted as I sped past the butcher counter.

"No, baby, not today." I steered the cart up to the checkout.

"Ma'am, you can't buy that cheese." The clerk's star-spangled acrylic nail tapped the WIC card. "See, it says right here. No organic allowed." She slid the folder across to me with a flick of her nail.

"But, it's on sale. It's the same price as the regular cheese."

The clerk stared at me, blew a pink gum bubble, and then flipped a switch. The light above the cashier's station started to flash. Bob the manager stared from behind the bulletproof glass; it took him a while to come out.

"Miss. You can switch the cheese or pay for it." He pointed to the brochure. "See? No organic allowed. We can't ring that up."

"Mami, pee pee," Maria said.

I didn't hear. I imagined making Maria and Nereida a quesadilla with organic cheese, a melting hot treat for breakfast. Something healthy for them, I thought. I asked again, even though I felt my throat, hot and scratchy.

"I guess I could switch it, but it's the same price as the other."

The line behind me was four deep. A woman with stark black roots and the protruding false pregnancy of middle age glared.

"Jesus Christ," the woman spat. She held two loaves of Wonder Bread and a single gallon of milk. "Can't we move this along?"

The manager and the gum-smacking cashier examined my order.

"What kind of juice is that?" They squinted at the WIC folder with its kindergarten-bright pictures of permissible cereals, carrots, peanut butter, milk, and beans. They matched each item on the belt with the coupons, piling the gallon of milk on top of the cereal box. I heard a crunching sound, but they stared at my one eight-ounce block of organic cheese. If I didn't get the right kind of cheese, I'd have to pay cash for it and lose the coupon anyway. I needed my three dollars to put some gas in the tank.

The line moved up. I felt the woman's breath almost in my ear.

"Jessie," the manager said, "go switch this cheese. We gotta get this line moving." Jessie rolled her eyes and sauntered toward the dairy section.

"Mami! Pee Pee!" It was no longer a warning. The smell of urine reached my nose, but we were trapped with angry people on both sides. Maria was crying, and Nereida's hat had slipped down over her eyes.

"Let's fix that." I took the hat off. Nereida's hair was plastered to her head with sweat. Jessie came back and slapped the cheese down on the conveyor belt. The manager registered my tired eyes and the girls' discomfort for the first time.

"Next time remember. No organic anything. It says so right on the folder. Save you some time."

He didn't say, "Waste less of everybody's time," but I read it in his eyes before we escaped to the cool air of the parking lot. I breathed in twilight and snow with grateful breaths.

"Okay, *niñas*, one more car trip. Look at the snow!"

"Ooooooh." Maria must have been uncomfortable in her wet pants, but she never complained. Turning onto Vernor Highway took a long time, but finally we were on our way home, just a mile to go. I nosed the Mazda onto our street.

I saw a black SUV parked in the spot I had spent the better part of the afternoon shoveling out, and my kitchen chair, legs bent and splayed like a dead animal, tossed aside on the snowdrift. I took a deep breath and inched down the block until I found parking at the end, in front of the apartment building. The snow was untouched, so I gunned the motor and plowed in.

Maybe I'd just leave the Mazda there for a few days and wait for the snow to melt.

"Hey, Maria, we're home, come on out." Maria climbed into thigh-high snow and waited for me to pull out the car seat. It occurred to me that clipping and unclipping, zipping and unzipping, carrying and unloading measured much of my life. I'd all but forgotten that there were spaces in between.

Night had fallen, the snow cleaning the city with the ease of making a bed with line-dried sheets in midsummer. All was still. Hidden in the shadow of the dark brick hotel, I never noticed the pine's evergreen branches, fragrant and laden with snow, reaching over us like an old friend. Here on Detroit's most southwest, most industrial, most polluted corner, the tree lived, growing and rooted in the space it had made. I picked up Nereida's car carrier and took Maria's hand. The streetlight created a halo of snow, illuminating the outline of the sidewalk ahead, just enough light to get home.

Water

Elisa, 2005

Last winter the residents of a red-and-white house in Windsor, on the Canadian side of the Detroit River, enjoyed an unusually prosperous and happy time. One Elisa Sinnett, Detroit-side-of-the-river dweller, began a new religion, and their house became her shrine, its focal point. Every morning to brace herself for another day at the only job she could find when she came back to Detroit, she stopped at the Detroit Riverwalk. Elisa said her sincere prayers to the river and to her newest shrine, wishing she lived in Canada.

Then she would bow a little half-Namaste bow and make a sign of the cross for good measure to the shrine of the river, the little red-and-white house. The people who lived there had no idea of the love and energy poured their way every morning, but they were frequently heard to say, "That was a good winter, last winter."

*

I grew up in the Catholic Church, and the part that made the most sense to me was that we blessed ourselves with the holy water on the way out. The water had to be blessed by a priest before it was holy. I used to be so angry with my mother for saying she could bless the water just as well as the priest. I thought she was arrogant. I see now that what Mom really objected to was the unfairness—her anger directed at the priests, against the hierarchy, against the patriarchy. I didn't trust her anger. I didn't know how to say this when I was a child because I was afraid. But I can say it now. To me, water is already holy, with or without the priest. And I'm not afraid of my mother's anger anymore.

*

One summer my nine-year-old daughter and I swam in the Peconic Bay, a saltwater finger separating the north and south shores of Long Island, New York. Nereida and I wore life jackets, and we walked out a long way in the shallow bay. Then, holding hands, we let ourselves drift back to shore. I felt connected, buoyed up. And I remembered that we all come from the ocean. The ocean is my mother.

*

In El Salvador, during the civil war, we visited the marginalized communities, *las tomas de tierra*, or places where whole communities had marched and settled on vacant government land. It was very hot, and David and Janet were doing medical consultations. The other Lisa and I wandered around the small village of cardboard and tin homes, and, like a lot of Americans on peace delegations, we were unable to be of service, two pale ghosts, less useful to the community than a pair of toddlers.

A young girl in a blue dress came up to us, smiling, offering, inexplicably, two frosty glasses of water, clinking with ice cubes.

Our leaders had warned us against drinking the water in El Salvador.

"No thanks," we mimed. We didn't want to get cholera, diphtheria, mumps, measles, rubella, and chickenpox.

The little girl's smile disappeared.

Lisa and I walked around in the hot, hot sun for two more hours. Two ugly Americans, with no conscience other than self-preservation and maintaining a ridiculous code where we end up on the "greater than" side of every equation.

Back in the States we confessed to each other that in our dreams we have accepted that glass of water with two hands a thousand times.

Prayer Requests

Elisa and Cesar, 1997

During our marriage, Cesar and I would ride with the baby up to a small town in Michigan's thumb area whose biggest claim to fame was a swinging bridge and a nearby sugar mill. Memo, Cesar's brother, was a Methodist pastor, and we would drive up to the parsonage for Sunday dinners with the family once a month. Memo's father-in-law was also a pastor, and when we went to dinner, there would be a total of two Methodist pastors (both Harvard grads), two pastors' wives, and if you are allowed to count twice for different categories, often a total of four pastors' daughters, three pastors' sons, and a pastor's grandson. It was a collection of very well-dressed, well-behaved saints, and it was understood that Cesar would be questioned and counseled about his drinking problem.

My struggle to blend in and lend help in the kitchen was my counseling session. To cook Peruvian food with family members who have been cooking together for generations meant that they already knew what to do, and my clumsy attempts at "helping" were less than an average ten-year-old in their family was capable of doing. Compared to their small-boned beauty, I felt like a clod lumbering around the kitchen.

The parsonage, a house in a wooded neighborhood a few blocks from the church, was only an hour-and-a-half away from

Detroit's southwest side where we lived, but I felt as if we were in another country where nobody got dirty or complained. When we first started going up to Crossville, Cesar and I would laugh about how sixteen-year-old Margarita got in trouble for trying to straighten her hair and how funny Dania looked trying to cook in high heels.

But now it seemed there was nothing to joke about, and I could hardly remember the last time we laughed together. My only impulse was to escape the stuffy kitchen. I would offer to take out the garbage to the attached garage and make my escape, wandering through nearby fields and back yards until we could politely leave.

I walked past the empty playground and crossed over to the Catholic church. I tested the doors; unlocked, but I was afraid to go in. Somewhere there was a priest who I could talk to, someone who could grant me absolution for my sins, lift them from me as if they had never happened. I gazed longingly at the church door and the inset stained glass window—blood red, alabaster white, golden streams of light.

At the Methodist church, I could write down my sins on a prayer request card and seal them inside the offertory envelope tucked into the back of the dark wooden pew. I'm not much of a believer, but I'd always leave it anyway, signed with a phony name, inside the red faux leather—bound hymnal. I'd considered the list of options on the card—check one:

Give this card to the prayer team.

I want to talk to the pastor.

I wish to let Jesus into my life.

I want to join the church.

I always checked box one: Give this card to the prayer team. I had a compulsion to do this every time I stepped foot in a Protestant church, usually as an invited guest. I hadn't been to a Catholic Mass or gone to confession since I married Cesar; but every time I prayed with the Methodists, it was so tempting to write down my sins and leave them in the capable hands of a prayer team.

Sometimes I told the truth, leaving pieces of my soul lighter when I left. "I'm afraid to leave my husband, and my daughter witnessed him hurting me." I wrote that one often. Cesar's family must have known those were my words, but they never once suggested I break my penance. Part of me must have believed I deserved it.

As I sat on the steps of the Catholic church with my back to the door, I looked out over the countryside. I felt more at home outdoors than inside a church or a kitchen. I'd return to the parsonage through a cornfield, breathing in the sharp, clean smell of snow, frozen stalks crunching beneath my feet. It was open and bright, like the land around the camp where I worked two summers ago. I spent my days leading groups of boys through fields and woods and down Suckers Creek until we reached the lake. This cornfield was a wide bridge between a woods on one side and the back yards of identical prefab houses on the other. A billboard announced, "Oak Grove Condominiums: Second Phase Coming Soon." It was clear which side of the cornfield was going to win. I was passing through a refuge that would soon disappear.

My shoes were wet, and there were leaves caught in my hair when I returned. Cesar greeted me with an enraged glare.

"Why did you leave me with the baby? Do you know what that makes me look like?"

Maria was crawling around the floor with her cousins, babbling something that sounded like "gol, gol, gol!"

Doña Medina gave me a look that could have been pity or something else. She filled a tray with coffee to serve to the men while they watched TV. I tried to assume a modest demeanor, but my hands were shaking, and one of the coffees slopped over into the sugar bowl. I knew I would pay later for my infraction with Cesar's angry words, or even fists.

I dreaded leaving as much as I couldn't wait to leave. We had parked the car down the street on purpose so nobody would see me wrench open the bashed-in passenger door or Cesar reach for the flat-head screwdriver that was our ignition key.

The ride down I-94 was a relief, although it was better for me when Cesar was trying to exhibit good behavior in the holy house of saints. As soon as we got on the freeway, I untucked my blouse and unbuttoned the top two buttons, slipping off my shoes, flexing my toes. His hand reached over and pinched my leg hard. It would leave a bruise. I blinked back tears and said nothing. I knew better than to talk back or complain. On my last birthday, we had gone to a seafood house that shared a parking lot with a gentleman's club. It had all the style and charm of a wedding reception at a VFW hall; the waitresses swiveled their hips to move around high chairs and overcrowded tables, but dinner was cheap, and Cesar didn't order a drink. The tip should have been about four dollars, but Cesar wouldn't leave more than a dollar. I tried to explain how much 15 percent was, but he kept getting madder. So I dug three dollars from my own purse and slammed it down next to the pepper shaker. The couple at the next table looked up, and I felt Cesar freeze. When we got to the car he slapped me so hard I could feel the imprint on my face—a hot, raised Braille print of his hand. Then he started to drive faster.

I sobbed. "Shut up!" Cesar yelled, but I couldn't stop, and Maria was crying too. Cesar punched the accelerator to the floor, and we lurched forward until the Mazda was going 90 miles an hour down the side streets of Lincoln Park, Michigan.

I rubbed the back of my neck and remembered. This time I kept quiet, and mercifully, the baby slept.

When we got home, I hopped out and moved the chairs out of our parking space, and Cesar squeezed the car in between a Dodge and a banged-up low rider. Then he carried Maria up the stairs to our flat while I followed him with the diaper bag. He went into the bathroom and came out a few minutes later, hair combed, teeth brushed, and fresh cologne wafting. I had Maria in my arms, and he kissed her on the forehead. "I'm going out," he said. He shrugged back into his coat. We'd been home less than fifteen minutes, but for Cesar it probably seemed like years.

I used to try to follow him around when he went drinking with his friends. I'd cruise parking lots of clubs in the neighborhood trying to spot his yellow 4x4 Toyota pickup truck. There was Club Internaciónal where the latest touring groups would come. That was when I was pregnant with Maria. Then he began to drink in places with no cover charge, which in our neighborhood meant anybody could get in. I had to search the parking lots, places I would never dare enter.

I cruised the parking lot of the Blue Diamond, where a man had been followed home, rolled for his paycheck, and killed in the stairwell of his apartment. It turned out later that the people he was drinking with had murdered him. We lived close to El Chaparral, where Jose Iturralde was shot six times by the Detroit Police for taking his ID from his back pocket. That was the easiest spot to check. But by now, the truck had been sold and the money sent to his mother in safekeeping for him. Then Cesar took over the beat-up Mazda, and I couldn't drive anymore without him taking me. I guess I was happy to have an excuse to stop my lonely patrol. Now they didn't even go to bars. In the summer they drank in Chicho's garage or on Tito's back porch. But it was a Sunday in January, and he was wearing Calvin Klein. He probably was at Pilar's, the neighborhood *pupuseria*. Pilar served beer and the Salvadoran stuffed tortillas from her restaurant in the basement of her red brick home on Junction Avenue, and it was always a party. I wondered who the cologne was for this time.

Maria began to fuss, so I began to walk with her, patting her on the back. Nineteen steps from the front window of the apartment to the back door and the steps down to Luciano's apartment. Side to side. Six steps from one side of the dining room to the other. Hardwood floors and high ceilings, but nowhere to go. Next Sunday was Maria's baptism, but sometimes I didn't think I could live with Cesar another day. I walked over to the window. I knew there had to be something better. Just in case, I kept a diaper bag filled with Pampers, a can of formula, a pair of my sweats, two pairs of baby pajamas, $168, and our passports. I peered out through the Venetian blinds.

Caridad and Lisandra were in their dining room, laughing at something. A curly-haired man wearing glasses and holding a beer laughed, watching Caridad; if he turned his head a fraction, he could have seen me. Caridad was doing some kind of shimmy, dancing, in imitation of something on the TV. Maria began to squirm, so I dropped the blinds and set her in the crib.

Time was contained as if I were in a snow globe as I paced back and forth. When I checked the kitchen clock, only ten minutes had passed since Cesar had left. I walked over to where his work jacket was hanging. I buried my face in it and hugged it. It smelled like him and fresh air. I took it to bed with me. I'd lay down, just for a minute.

I woke and looked at the red LED display: 11:30. Maria was still asleep. I walked the length of the apartment and looked out the front window. A blanket of snow was covering the cars, softening the sharp edges and torn bumpers and dirty salt stains. It was hushed and calm. But no Cesar. I lay back down. The next time I woke with a start. Footsteps on the back stairs and a pounding on the back door. The clock read 1:45. He had to be drunk. I swung my legs out of bed. I wanted to push the bedroom door shut. Let him stay out in the street if that was where he was happiest. Let him want something he can't have for a change. But then Cesar started shouting and pounding louder, and I was afraid he was going to break the window. I hurried toward the back door, but Luciano from downstairs had gotten the spare key and was already letting him in.

Cesar lunged at me, slamming me into the kitchen door. He grabbed my head by the hair and held on so he could give me two *cachetadas*. My face felt like it was on fire. I put my hands up in front of me so he could only punch my arms. Why hadn't I put the chain on? Why hadn't I gone over to Caridad's? I'd known something bad was going to happen tonight, but something inside of me made me stay, made me let him in—the same feeling when I took a razor blade and cut Jackson's initials into my arm when I was in tenth grade. I looked up. Luciano's eyes glinted behind his glasses like a lizard waiting for a fly. He backed up and shut the door. I slumped down. Cesar looked at me and kicked me once, hard, on the upper thigh.

"*Pendeja*," he spat. "Who's the piece of *basura* on the floor now?" He wrenched the door to our bedroom and lay down on the bed. I didn't dare move until I heard his snore. Somehow Maria was still sleeping. I walked to the couch and curled into a ball. The rays from the streetlamp were shining in the window like a child's night light, and finally I fell asleep.

*

Baptism. Seven days had passed, and it was Sunday again. On the seventh day we would rest. On that day, Maria would be baptized with the Holy Spirit and her sins erased. She would belong to the body of Christ and be a member of the Iglesia Metodista Unida. Cesar wore a tie, and Maria's gown hung in the car. The family waited at the church. We drove up, and already the best parking spots were taken. It was filling up: regular Sunday service followed by a special Baptism ceremony and then breakfast in the church basement. We took our seats and opened our hymnals.

> *Come you sinners poor and needy*
> *Weak and wounded, sick and sore,*
> *Jesus ready stands to save you*
> *Full of pity, love and power.*

The service was almost over, and it was time to take Maria and change her into her baptismal gown. I dressed her. She looked like a tiny Mayan doll, but the long white baptismal gown seemed wrong. I looked into her dark eyes. She returned my gaze steadily with a look older than time. She already was blessed and didn't need forgiveness. She needed nothing from this place, and I was surprised to discover that neither did I. Clutching her to me, I hurried to the car without our coats on. I buckled her in and reached for the screwdriver to turn the ignition—to drive toward water. True water. Blue Water Bridge, Port Huron, and then farther north to Lexington. I was returning to a place where nobody could find me.

*

The chapel at the summer camp shared its small white building with the supply shed, and the spare key was still where I used to hide it. I didn't feel like a trespasser as I entered through the storage area. The sleeping bags and tents were stacked; fishing poles and even an old work jacket were still there. I draped the jacket around Maria and made my way through the inner door. There were two wooden pews and an altar. Framed pictures drawn by children decorated the walls, and the happy, smiling, Crayon stick angels surrounded me. There were objects laid before the altar too: five stones, stalks of wheat, a piece of birch bark, and a candle, its wax still soft and warm.

I took Maria out into the birch grove. The white trunks were bare that day, but they carried in them the possibility of leaves and the memory of children playing tag before dinner. I saw footprints leading to the lake trail. I shifted Maria on my hip and pulled the jacket tighter. We walked to the trailhead and looked over the tree line to the water below, gray and infinite. She smiled at me, and her eyes held a dangerous secret. It was enough.

Something You Build: Detroit

For Alexis and Jamie, 2015

Jamie's not a little girl anymore, not trapped in a tiny, hot room with mewling puppies and no exit. Jamie doesn't get a fictional rescue from that room by her teenage stepsisters and the author of this story who doesn't believe that Jamie ever got out. Jamie lives. Jamie gets to farm the land, starts the Green Revolution, before the first- and the second-wave hipsters who came because they thought that Detroit was empty, void, fallow, there for the taking and the raping.

Jamie pulls aside the back curtain, gossamer white with tiny blue flowers. She sees Orlando in the back feeding the chickens. Orlando is real; he's not that cute boy from seventh-grade science class who died in his twenties. He's standing next to the chicken coop, built alongside the red brick one-car garage, almost to the back alley. This chicken coop isn't the one where the author's mother grew up, a half-dozen siblings, hungry and cold, in a thin, tar paper shack. This is the kind of chicken shack that keeps actual chickens warm, and Jamie's husband is alive in a future neither one of them ever lived. His breath is coming out in small white puffs, and here in mid-October, the trees are putting on a show with the bright colors of the bejeweled Michigan autumn. Jamie places her hand over her stomach as she leans in, her breath fogging the window. She wipes it off with her sleeve and then raps on the window to get her husband's attention. She mouths the word "coffee" and mimics drinking from a cup.

I'll leave you here, to see these Detroiters who stayed, alive and well and building things. It could happen. Some people stay, but I believe they are haunted by ghosts of dead friends, relatives, lovers. They stay, and fight, and build. Don't judge me too harshly for leaving. Say a prayer for me, please. Bring this to your prayer teams, even though I don't deserve it. I committed White flight when they divided the school system into three and declared open season on longtime Detroiters.

"Be right in, Jamie," he shouts, giving her a thumbs up.

She can see Orlando rolling up the hose and hanging it back on the rain barrel, done with watering their pumpkin patch in the lot next door. Sometimes she wonders how she, a spindly White girl with cigarette burns on her arms, ended up with this beautiful light-skinned Black man from the rich side of town. The field bursts with globes of orange, and this year's harvest festival would bring out kids from the neighborhood to choose the best one for jack-o'-lantern carving. Jamie pulls the teakettle off the small cooktop and pours it over the ground coffee with precision. Orlando opens the door and pulls off his boots.

He gives Jamie a warm kiss, his large hand resting lightly on the back of her neck. "Mm mm," he says, reaching out for his cup of coffee.

"Let's go to the front porch," she suggests and shrugs into an oversized sweater.

They sit on the steps in silence. This block reminds her of the one she grew up on in southwest Detroit with its one-way streets and lack of driveways, but she knows it's what happens on the inside of a house that counts. Jamie's early childhood was terrifying. Orlando never forgets this. He squeezes her knee.

"So what are you thinking?"

"That it's an inside job. You know, change is an inside job." This is what she tells the women when they come to the therapy group at the shelter where she's a counselor.

"I bet they don't believe that," Orlando replies.

"Not at first," Jamie says. "Not until they feel safe enough to believe that they can change their situation." She's silent for a moment. "I was just thinking about the therapy group. I got a text this morning that there was a new intake on the substance abuse side." She loves how Orlando listens not only to what she's saying, but is also in tune to what she thinks.

"So...maybe you're a little worried?" he asks.

She knows he's saying something else too; he means: "Do you need anything from me?"

Orlando waits and listens as she gathers her thoughts.

"Sometimes I feel like I have to gear up a little, be on my guard." Jamie takes another sip of coffee. Across the street and down to the far corner, the dwarf apple orchard that Orlando and the neighborhood kids planted three years ago is maturing. For two years the blossoms seemed to bloom and die with very little fanfare. But this year, their third, with the beehives positioned in the middle of the orchard, the flowers have produced the miracle of apples. Hopefully they'll be ready for the harvest festival and candy apples for the children.

Orlando is a physician like his father, and he goes to the clinic four days a week. The rest of the time he works on his favorite project—making their block and four of the neighboring blocks a model for urban life. Orlando grew up in Detroit's best neighborhood, Palmer Woods, but everyone in his family saw the whole picture of Detroit, not just their giant houses and shady streets.

Orlando trusted Jamie from the moment they met because she didn't treat him like a celebrity. She had never heard of his model mother or his famous twin sister. She didn't know what a trust fund was, and instead of being impressed with it, she had suggested to Orlando that he should go back to school and add a horticulture degree so he could see his dream of self-sustaining neighborhoods come to life.

Jamie knows that the women in the center count their days clean, and the timing of the group sessions is crucial. For most of them, it is a matter of life and death.

"I should go," she says. "I wish I had time for another cup of coffee."

"Okay, then, but here's maybe something better." Orlando pulls an apple from his pocket. "It's a Pink Lady. They're ready to harvest." Orlando drains his coffee and kisses her, setting his empty cup next to hers. The red skin of the apple glows, blessing their morning and their goodbyes.

Jamie bikes, inhaling the crisp fall air. She sails under the canopy of bright leaves and brakes at the far corner of the orchard before she continues her ride. This small detour was her real reason for not staying and finishing her coffee. Orlando was right; the apples were glinting red in the morning light like so many jewels. The harvest festival was going to be a big hit this year with free hayrides and treats for the kids.

She stands astride her bicycle in silence and holds the vision of the fruitful orchard in her heart, proof that new life can survive here, despite the destruction that the newcomers have brought to the neighborhoods and the schools.

Jamie pedals over to the orchard gate, closes her eyes, and breathes in. She imagines Orlando lifting the heavy log and swinging it out as the children rush in—running through the pumpkin patch or finding the fairy lights leading them into the trees. The newest Detroiters will fill baskets with apples, amid plenty and celebration, as the days head toward the longest night and the world points away from the sun.

Mother, We Were So Close When You Were Choking Me: Elisa

Elisa and Marie, 2019

"Hi, Mama." That's what Nereida, my eighteen-year-old, says to me.

"Hi, Mom," says Maria, her big sister, a little older, more sophisticated.

What shall I call you? Mama, Mom, Ma? Mother? Mommy?

My sisters are convinced you still speak to us. You send dimes. Dimes with inflation, not pennies from heaven. Even my sister the atheist is encouraged by these missives in the form of dimes being placed under glue-on tiles as they ready the porch where Dad will sit. Dimes in the attic, as we clean out garbage, preparing our family home in Detroit for sale. Dimes on the kitchen table when we help Claire, Dad's wife.

"Dimes," they say, looking at each other with raised eyebrows.

"Dimes," they say. Mom is watching. Mom approves. These messages from the divine, my mother pitching diamonds over the heavenly right field wall, are enough for them.

Today, I got a two-dollar bill in change from the man at the booth for Hampshire Farms at the Royal Oak Farmer's Market. At another, the Sweet Potato Pie booth, I bought two pies with the change and almost spent the two-dollar bill, but held it out toward Nereida instead. The Black man selling the sweet potato pies said, "Today I gave out ten two-dollar bills. I wondered where they got to."

I showed him the bill; he nodded as I handed it to Nereida. "For good luck."

Was that you, Mom? Are you a Black baker now? I'd like to imagine you happy, baking pies, passing out two-dollar bills just because. My other mother, sociology professor Max Heirich, died a year ago today.

He was always a bit worried for me. He caught me, but there has always been too much of me for anyone to catch.

I'm still hungry, looking for you. But I'm not sure what's wrong with me that a dime isn't enough. Ten two-dollar bills and sweet potato pie with a sweet eighteen-year-old who calls me "Mama" is enough now, because it's what I have, and we have been taught to appreciate our daily bread.

I can thank you for that, for the "Our Father who art in heaven" and "Give us this day our daily bread" and "Hail Mary" and the "Lord is my shepherd," but they're words in a vast silence of profound loneliness.

When we were small, on hot nights we all slept on the floor near the air conditioner in your room.

As we pack up my childhood home now, this room is the hardest to see empty. This was the only cool room in the house. I remember this room when we were sick. It became a sick room with mumps and measles and fevers and chickenpox. I brought cups of chocolate milk to my sisters when they were sick, and it was my job to be the fifth child to catch the disease. It was real chocolate milk. I remember your vanity dresser with its small collection of perfume and costume jewelry.

I don't know you, Mom. I never did. The room where you slept is empty.

There's a glass of sour chocolate milk, a space on the floor next to my sisters, and a stuffed toy cat with real fur and a missing leg that nobody can touch in the very back of your closet. But you're not here. You have a wet towel over your head. There's a message on the answering machine about a group for rape and incest survivors. You say it must have been a wrong number. I look for you everywhere, but you're not here.

There's the back of your nightgown, you're walking into the bathroom and shutting a door. A jumble of pill bottles in the cabinet. You're cooking and humming, but we can't talk to you. Oh, I sought an opening my whole life.

Once you landed on me and choked me; you were so close, our breaths mingled. We were so close when you were choking me.

After the brain surgery, you couldn't get enough of us, and the last years of your life you saw only my back. It wasn't on purpose. Your hand was grasping me, pulling me back, but we had never been anywhere. I never could find you, and then when you wanted me, there was no common ground to return to, not even a dime's worth.

"Bye, Mama"

Elisa and Marie, 2012

This will be a very short story.

"Bye, Mama."

People will like to hear the goodbye story. She had a bad fall. An ambulance took her to the hospital. She went into a coma. She was alone when she went into the coma because we thought she was going to get better because she always got better. We were going to see her in the morning. She said good night. I said good night. We would see her tomorrow. She was safe. She was in the hospital. She said good night, and sometime in the night, she lost consciousness, and she never woke up.

She gave us time to go, to fly in, drive in, walk in. We tried to call Jolene, her best friend from the old days, to let her talk to Mom one more time, to hold the phone up to her ear. We knew Jolene was the one to call because Mom flew to visit Jolene in California on her fiftieth birthday, and Mom was terrified of airplanes. But when we called Jolene, she couldn't talk because she, too, was in a coma. And then Jolene died.

At the hospital, everyone went in one by one to say a private goodbye to Mom before the nurses disconnected the machines. Everyone but me.

All of us, all six of her daughters, were gathered around her bedside. She had no tubes or wires. We sang to her; we all touched her, healing hands, singing her home. I, the daughter who apparently had no discernable talents, was the one who felt the shift.

"It's time to sing 'Amazing Grace,'" I said. When we were the Sinnett Family Singers, we performed this song in the nursing homes. We each got a verse. Mine was always, "The Lord is my shepherd, I shall not want, he leads me down to lie, in pastures green he leadeth me, the quiet waters by."

We sang "Amazing Grace." People said there were heavenly angels in the room.

She stopped breathing on my verse, but I did not say goodbye.

When she was alive, I asked her once, "Mom, why don't you like me?"

She didn't hesitate. "You're just like your dad's family. You look just like his sister. You act just like him."

Is there a question I should be asking? Is there something you know that I don't know? I am missing pieces of myself, and I don't know where to find them.

She didn't hesitate. I didn't say goodbye.

Bye, Mama.

Elegy for Our Home in Detroit

Elisa, Nereida, Maria, 2014

I'm sorry if I seem a little scattered since the hipster invasion of Detroit; I've lost a few things, and if you can find them, will you send them my way?

I've lost: two peach trees, one pear tree, one plum tree, five rose bushes, one fairy door, one swing set (used), one playscape (pirates and adventurers since moved on), one wall mural, one door frame with ten years of my daughters' growth marked in permanent marker, and yes, what I really want back are those years.

It was all eternity, but now we have been displaced.

In the house that you live in, in the city you declare bankrupt, in the school system you have dismantled, you have stolen our memories.

I miss my home. I grieve the house we lived in when the children were small, the rooms they pulled their stuffed animals through by a long ear or a string, those marks on the door frame to show how they've grown, because we were never going to leave.

Here are the rooms of the nine hundred square feet and the happiest days of my life: hardwood floors, high ceilings with crown mouldings in a fleur-de-lis pattern, stained glass windows, and a crystal chandelier. We painted the front room blue, the color Nereida chose. "Blue like my dress, Mami. *Azul! Azul*, Mami!" She ran up to me on the couch saying her name is Esther and that she would crown her big sister the queen of all the cheetahs.

The neighbor girl, Itzlali, painted the dining room a soft green, and it resembles a room from a magazine with the bronze chandelier and the long white curtains, but then I put in the toys and art supplies and a rug. It becomes a place of ever-changing landscapes, and there Maria and Nereida spend hours; they sing, dress up, marry each other, and their stuffed animals become involved in long fairy stories from bright picture books.

The best days are the days after the trial when Cesar has been released and has already gone away to Honduras. Those moments are the sweetest, when the evening is hushed.

Soon it will be time to lay Maria and Nereida down in their toddler beds in the room with the mural that Itzlali painted. Fairy creatures from Mexico come alive at night and bring the girls into a nighttime world populated with one-eyed birds and bright colored flowers the size of their heads. "Mami, sing us another song," the girls say, and I do, the one about the coyote.

And perhaps snowflakes fall from the sky, and Detroit quiets; my bedroom looks out onto the back yard, where the snow covers the playscape, the fruit trees, the garden fence.

Maybe I hear the back door open and shut, and the family that lives upstairs pops their heads in through the kitchen door; Patrice and her two children, Juan and Salome.

"I'll get the kids up to bed," she says. And soon my housemate and friend from the old neighborhood comes down the stairs, and we share coffee or a drink and whisper plans for our children, dreams for things we are going to do. She shows me her timeline to quit the Detroit EMS and become a midwife; I promise to look into classes to get my teaching certificate. Maybe we can get the kids into that new art school.

At night the Detroit sky still flames red in brilliant sunsets from the upstairs back porch, and the trees grow peaches and pears and plums in the summer, and the roses the Lithuanian woman planted wind through the fences in a pink, white, and red barricade. I pick two dozen red roses on the last day of school in the migrant center where I am the teaching assistant and give each graduating mother a rose for completing the ESL course. But at the end of the year, we are all laid off, and we have to reinterview for our own jobs.

I wear my mother's clothes to the interview, a long, two-piece sweater dress with low-heeled loafers. They still smell like her, lavender and fresh sheets. I resemble a round owl with tortoiseshell glasses, not even curvaceous, just round. I miss her, or maybe it's just the illusion of having someone on my side. Mom always rooted for the underdog, even if it was me.

As I walk in, I feel a chill invading my body. The principal interviewing me is an iguana; his tongue slips in and out of his moist lips. The union representative at the meeting exchanges a look with the principal, lifts his eyebrows. When I leave, past the large glass windows of the interview room, I can see their heads bent together. The secretary, a woman my age dressed in a tight leather pantsuit and four-inch heels, walks into the room. The men smile at her. She asks a question or says something, and they laugh. I don't get the job, and everyone in our center is replaced by a Teach for America volunteer.

I find a job where I fit in. I work at Wendy's; the smock is blue and white, and it makes me look slimmer. My coworkers don't look down on me, and because of my freckles, some of them even call me Wendy. I'm one of the fastest cashiers, they say. "That's pretty good," I say. There is no history, just me tying on my blue-and-white headscarf in the bathroom at Wendy's hamburgers.

I can make change by counting backwards, so I know if the computer is wrong. I never needed a calculator to do math. I can just open the cash register with a key and count out the change; because I can do math fast in my head, I get the best shifts. When the line is nine deep, I like to catch someone's eyes in the back, see their hungry look, and watch their surprise when they get all the way up to the front in no time. It also means I get to talk to whole football teams, people who would never talk to me when I was in high school—they are filled with gratitude when they get their orders.

Square beef slabs, pink and plump, stacked on their paper squares, line the walk-in shelves until it's time to carry them over to the grill. I know how to work every station, the register, the grill, the Frosty machine, the fryers, and the cleanup stations— pots and pans, mopping, scrubbing the bricks, vacuuming, window washing. My apron is caked with grease when I work the grill, and when I close the restaurant, I have sweated and cooled down so many times throughout my shift I feel like an athlete, both spent and high on endorphins.

The giant stainless steel lettuce chopper is the only machine that I edge away from. I told my bosses all those shiny little blades were too much for me. I wanted to see what my arm would look like chopped into little squares; I've always liked blades. Maybe I shouldn't have said that out loud. Maybe that's why I've never made manager, even though I said, "Just kidding."

How do I lose the house? It happens in stages. Wendy's doesn't pay that well, and Cesar is back and in and out of the house; I can't get him to move out. Then one night Cesar starts a fight in the bar; two guys drag him outside, throw him down on the ground, and start kicking him in the head. His cousin stabs one of the guys and is arraigned for attempted murder. His cousin saved Cesar's life; I take the money out of the house to pay for the lawyer and his cousin's freedom. But I am finally able to tell Cesar to go to hell, and he mostly stays away. I think he's met someone. Zunilda. They move back to Cesar's family farm in Honduras. That's what I hear from his cousins.

Then the storm rips half of the roof off, and the house loan pays for the contractor who fixes the roof, but he doesn't fix it. Kent threatens to kill me when I try to get my money back. Don't ever use Kent's Roofing in Detroit. Fuck you, Kent. Your dad is rolling over in his grave for what you did to his business, you motherfucker.

"Your kids like to play in the back yard, don't they?" he says. And the next day the back gate is missing from the yard. And so the house loan pays for a new gate and bars on the window, and another guy, a neighbor, to slap some tar on the roof to hold it together for the winter, and a floor and ceiling for the upstairs kitchen, ruined by the roof that Kent built. It's like Stephen King started writing nursery stories and implanting them into people's yards in Detroit, and you can't return the book to the library because the library's been burned down.

There's always a place for money to go, until I start having to buy the food with the credit card again, because one thing about Cesar being in Honduras is that he's in Honduras, not here, and the girls need shoes and winter coats.

So we get behind, and then we get behind some more. Patrice, who rents the upstairs rooms, gives birth to Emma, and then Patrice moves out to the east side into her new boyfriend's place. Things fall apart little by little. My house goes to someone with $17,000 to spare. I'm not allowed to buy my house for $17,000, but someone else can. The couple is bright-eyed with glee. The woman laughs and takes a picture of the sales price. "You have to post that. They won't believe what a steal they can get here," he says. He doesn't pronounce the "r;" they're not from around here. They barely glance at me.

I start selling the furniture. The one-bedroom apartment we can rent in the town just north of Detroit doesn't have room for all of the bookshelves and dressers. I keep the table from the house I grew up in, the one we made with Dad, and the girl's bunk beds. I keep Mom's blue mixing bowl and the girls' art supplies and dressup clothes. As I pack the last box in the truck, I sniff new adventure too.

The girls are bewildered by the silence in the suburbs. They learn how to cross the street. They learn how to ride their bikes. They are ten and twelve when we move out of Detroit, and their babyhood is gone, forever in the house on Larkins Street, on the dead-end block where we climbed down onto the freeway with jugs of water for the truckers the day the traffic stopped and the power grid went out on the entire Eastern Seaboard.

I want to write a new history for myself. I do not know the name of my great-grandmother. It is as if a giant hand deposited us here, lifted from the nothing, a myth of a place over the ocean; always within a few miles of the narrow place in the river called Detroit.

Michigan, from space, is in the shape of a mitten; it is a left hand, left-handed like me. The narrow strait between Detroit and Canada curves around what would be the thumb joint; the rest of the state is filled with trees and people who are sure that Jesus is White and wants us to bomb the infidels. The talking heads on the TV say that what happens now is what matters, and what came before is nobody's fault who is alive today, and we should forget it.

I look in the mirror to see if there are answers to the history written there, but I see nothing. If I stare at myself long enough, my eyes will start to scare me. I believe there is something you can see in eyes, and that is what we see into other people, but myself? I keep seeing an attic behind me filled with trunks and boxes, things of value peeping out: velvet, wooden, and silver, entire rooms, lifetimes of treasures, carried over from other places and other times, carried in the holds of ships, treasures stolen from the manor houses, traded in exchange for safe passage to another place. This room is full of stolen pickings.

I would have lost the house anyway; I am glad that the one peach tree still bears fruit. The new couple that lives there tore down the playhouse and built a fire pit. I drove through the alley just to see; it was dusk. They took the pear tree out too and laid cement down. I stepped out of my car, and I could hear laughing. I peered around the garage and the new bike shed. I smelled a strong odor of weed. They painted over the graffiti on the garage, and the tall grass and the grape vines are gone. I wonder what would happen if I introduced myself to them. If I told them that they are standing on hallowed ground; it used to belong to us, and we to it. I know that this story has happened to people over and over again in history, that the owners will never see who I really am through the smoke of their campfire.

But there is a bigger universe than I can see, and what happens down here doesn't alter that. The change has already happened, and there is enough to remind me of this under the moon and in the morning below the day-blind stars.

But I miss my home.

I miss the baskets of peaches in the summer and the long days on the back porch when my children were small.

Literary Acknowledgments

Detroit Fairy Tales. YesYes Books Fiction Contest finalist

"The View from Senator Street." *Woven Tale Press*, October 2019 featured artist spotlight

"Mother, We Were So Close When You Were Choking Me." *Hip Mama Magazine*, 2018

"Prologue Detroit 1967: What They Were Told." *Mutha Magazine*, November 2017

"Mother's Milk." Honorable Mention, *Hip Mama*-Unchaste Readers Writing Contest, 2015

"Elegy for Our Home in Detroit." *Hip Mama Magazine*, 2014

"No Organic Allowed." *Stealing Time Magazine*, 2013

"Meant to Disturb." *Penduline Press*, also nominated for Best of the Net 2012

"Park." "On the Fly." The Lit Star Collective, 2009

"Penthouse Living." *Glimmer Train* New Writer Award finalist, 2008

"Driving to El Salvador with Hector and Domingo." *Friends Journal*, Associated Church Press Award of Excellence, 2006

Acknowledgments

To my fellow readers of independent literature, thank you for your part in bringing this book into being: publisher/editor/author/mentor and friend William E. Burleson, Chelsey Clammer, Dr. Claire Crabtree, Ariel Gore, Helen Weaver Horn, Olivia Pandolfi, and the Wayward Writers. Thanks and love to my dear ones, especially Nora Romelia Sinnett, Dyani Armijo-Sinnett, and Steve Deasy. Love and gratitude for my way back other sisters Elizabeth Cadena, Debranne Dominguez and Heather Robinson, To my family and extended family especially Dennis Sinnett, Peggy Sinnett, Jeanne Flynn, Barb Zacharczyk, Jennifer Miltenburg, Patty Bruni and Kathleen Sinnett. Gratitude to the people and places who held us steady: the ancestors, the trees, Hubbard Farms, Larkins Street, Gesu Parish, Early Head Start, (Avancemos!) Detroit Head Start, WIC, the Acosta Center, American Indian Health and Family Services, Safe House, Sheila Johnson, the Ferndale Mamas especially Nicole Smith. Cynthia Mitchell and Karen Twomey, the Ferndale Golden Eagles Marching Band, Detroit Friends Meeting and the Ann Arbor Friends Meeting. To Hamtramck High School.

To Detroit.

About the Author

Elisa Sinnett is an immigrant to the middle class and was dismayed to discover shortly after her arrival that it was being dismantled. She enjoys life on her severely curtailed teacher's salary and is a member of the American Federation of Teachers. She lives in Windsor, Ontario, with her family across the river from her original hometown of Detroit, Michigan. She admires writers, activists, dreamers, peacemakers, and fellow teachers who are hanging in there for public education.

She works on her writing with author Ariel Gore and the Literary Kitchen. Selections of her book *Detroit Fairy Tales* have been published in and/or recognized by YesYes Books, *Hip Mama Magazine, Mutha Magazine, The Woven Tale Press, Penduline Press, Glimmer Train, Stealing Time Magazine,* and *Friends Journal. Detroit Fairy Tales* is her first book.

www.elisasinnett.com

About the Artwork

 Santa Fe-based artist Debranne Dominguez is best known for her primitive magical realism paintings. The subject matter is influenced by Latino folklore and childhood memories from 1970s Detroit. Find out more: www.elisasinnett.com

CPSIA information can be obtained
at www.ICGtesting.com
Printed in the USA
LVHW010234280821
696293LV00006B/1041

9 781733 976381